WORKING AT
SWINDON
WORKS
1930  1960

WORKING AT
SWINDON
WORKS

1930 GWR 1960

PETER TIMMS

TEMPUS

To my parents who, fifty years ago, had to make that decision –
Stevenage, Harlow New Town or Railway Swindon.

Front cover, top: Crane men. Left to right: -?-, Vic, Corbett, -?-, Sam Jones, Fred Archer and Jack Bates. The 'Triangle', Swindon, on 22 July 1962. (R. Grainger)

Front cover, below: Swindon Works' most famous product, *King George V*, unusually photographed by the company in day-to-day working conditions *c.*1947. (BR National Railway Museum)

First published 2007

Tempus Publishing
Cirencester Road, Chalford,
Stroud, Gloucestershire, GL6 8PE
www.tempus-publishing.com

Tempus Publishing is an imprint of NPI Media Group

British Library Cataloguing in Publication Data.
A catalogue record for this book is available from the British Library.

ISBN 978 0 7524 4403 1

Typesetting and origination by NPI Media Group
Printed in Great Britain

CONTENTS

INTRODUCTION

There are inevitably some areas of this subject which have been missed or not covered sufficiently. This is because either the information did not come my way in time or I chose not to repeat what has been published before. The 1930s–50s is the period that is of the greatest interest to me and I think to most people as well. Many locals knew people 'inside' during that time and it is happily still in living memory for a few ex-employees. This is not to say that the years prior to 1930 were insignificant – they were not. After the 1950s the Works became just another repair centre for a railway system in decline, and the things that made Swindon Works great had gone by the end of the decade.

Swindon was not the birthplace, nor headquarters, of the Great Western Railway (GWR): it was the manufacturing centre. However, it is usually the first place that comes to mind when people think of the great company. Swindon Works was a part of the Chief Mechanical and Electrical Engineer (CME) Department, and where this study inevitably overlaps the department's other work I have included details. Only the resident Stores Department and the Central Laundry were not part of the CME Dept. Of the staff employed in the department, 33 per cent were at Swindon Works in 1930, although this figure was down by 1932 and remained between 25 and 28 per cent until the late 1950s. Large numbers of railway workers were also were employed at the nearby Junction Station and the Motive Power Department – both outside the scope of this book. Up until 1916 the department was called the Loco, Carriage & Wagon Department. The company continued to use the old title on some documents right up to the 1930s. The public face of the Western, the equipment they used and services provided reached a peak as early as the 1930s. This was not the case with the pay and conditions of its servants. Both had to improve, and this they did over the two following decades. The company also invested heavily in manufacturing and paybill technology at Swindon. The 1930s may have become known as 'the heyday' or 'zenith' of the GWR but behind the publicity internal and external matters conspired against them. The company survived the economic depression remarkably well and history has been kind about its record during the Second World War, but this should not detract from the scale of difficulties they faced.

The management and Board of Directors at Paddington were not concerned with the conditions of their factory workers. If the conditions were unacceptable, workers were free to leave any time they chose to. In the late nineteenth century, any offers to co-operate with the men were no more than attempts to frustrate the organisation of trade unionism. This attitude hastened the establishment of the Factories Act and galvanised the workers into organising themselves in the workplace. However, where they could still exert power the bosses showed little regard for the men even in more enlightened times. When asked to intervene to

Aerial view of the Works with the CME's offices in the centre. (BR National Railway Museum)

The Works' principle officers in 1930. Standing left to right: S.J. Smith, R.G. Hannington, J. Kelynack, and E.T.J. Evans. Sitting left to right: J.R.W Grainge, J. Auld, C.B. Collett, F.W. Hawksworth and F.C. Hall. (BR National Railway Museum)

moderate the numbers of dismissals at Swindon, the chairman of the GWR, Viscount Horne, said, 'this is how the company works and these men knew that when they were hired'. This, of course, was quite right and proper but he could have questioned why so many men were given notice when all the signs were that industry was coming out of recession. By the 1930s a few hard-fought concessions had been secured; however, the Great Western ran a successful business and could not have been so prosperous by being more benevolent towards its servants, given the conditions of those times. This makes the early Swindon idea all the more fantastic, that if you allow for the medical, educational and spiritual welfare of the workers, they might just serve you better.

Information about the day-to-day work and remuneration of the senior managers of the period was never recorded outside the railway and by the time researchers took an interest these people had long since passed on. Similarly, the Great Western knew there was no publicity value in the work done by the senior clerk or the organisation of their department. The massive task of producing the individual paybill accounts for all the workers in the department had become fully mechanised by the early 1930s. Twenty-five years later the best possible methods of processing the accounts, and in particular paybills, given the short time span, was still a top priority. This is why one of the first computers to be used in industry was installed in the Works. The GWR employed the best technology available for its wages production. Had the GWR chosen not to se such pioneering equipment any other system would have failed to even interest the railway press and the historian could be forgiven for thinking the whole subject unremarkable. Of the period, 1937 was a good year for the company but there was a large increase in the cost of salaries and wages. For every £1 taken in receipts, they paid out 11*s* in salaries, wages and personal expenses. This was not only the largest single expenditure, it was larger than all other costs put together. The annual wages bill for the CME Dept was around £6.5 million. They could not afford to be unremarkable in their methods of wages production.

Many different, yet interchangeable, terms were used by Swindonians to describe their employer, including the Railway, the Company, the Western, the Factory, 'inside' and, of course, the GWR. Their random use hereafter serves to emphasise how equally common they all were.

Acknowledgements and Sources

Initially, I recorded the recollections from my friends and ex-railwaymen, John (Jack) Fleetwood and George (everyone knows George) Petfield. As I was then mainly concerned with all aspects of wages, I met some of the former forgotten army of the offices; in particular, Dr Barbara Carter (*née* Dening), Yvonne Hodey (*née* Jones), Liz Bartlett (*née* Ribbins) and Enid Hogden (*née* Warren). When I moved on to research conditions the following contacted me, all keen to help: Harry Bartlett, John Brettell, Bert Harber, Alan Lambourn, Peter Reade, Gordon Turner, Dave Viveash and Doug Webb. Thank you all for your time and enthusiasm. Thank you Richard Clarke, the late Ken Ellis, Tony Huzzey, David Lewis, Ronnie Lambourn, John Nutty, Brian Smithson, Richard Woodley, Anne Sweeney, Beryl Wynn (*née* Odey), as well as reporters at the *Swindon Advertiser*. Thank you Dianne Timms for your typing and computer skills, particularly retrieving irreplaceable text from cyberspace, and to Amy Rigg and Sophie Atkins at Tempus. Thanks also to Peter Trewin and others at British Railways Board (Residuary) Ltd for allowing me to use official photos in my own collection and in the Swindon Reference Library.

I have been fortunate to have met hundreds of local railway staff over the years in my work and as a collector of railway books and documents, and have mixed in some of their stories too. Alas, it is getting more difficult these days to obtain reliable first-hand accounts from ex-railway staff that go back to when the company name could be truly applied. There are certain myths that have evolved about the GWR factory. For instance, most writers and ex-railway staff sum up the old days as 'hard but fair'. Health and safety measures were, they say, 'non-existent', and when referring to the product manufactured, 'no expense was spared' is another overgeneralisation. Above all, it is felt that the company they, and invariably their fathers, had worked for was an 'excellent employer'. Having studied the subject from a variety of sources, I believe that the memory is indeed selective. I respect the fact that these people were there and I was not, but I think writing, based on recollections alone, could be misleading. It is wise to cross-reference technical details wherever possible and while I am reasonably confident with them, the memories herein must be classed as unverifiable. Alfred Williams's eloquent study of human predicament in the factory was written when events were fresh in his mind, and here perhaps lies its true value.

The staff of the Swindon Reference Library were very helpful. The library is a wonderland of local history and a humbling experience for anyone thinking that this subject is easily manageable. The staff magazines, at least those from before 1948, are the best kept records of this railway's social and professional activities, and are less affected by the bias aimed at the general public. For me, the best publication is the short-lived *Swindon Railway News* of the early 1960s – full of reflective snippets about characters, practices and incidents. Other publications containing material now unobtainable anywhere else are the various transactions of the Swindon Engineering Society presented by members of the Works' staff during that period. I have studied company rule books, just as every employee was required to do, as well as instruction books that were once kept in every office for 'ensuring uniformity of practice and procedure'. Certain engineering and operational details have been checked using textbooks once belonging to the last two heads of department of the old company. The railway trade unions provided handbooks for the various sections of workers detailing conditions of service, and surviving copies proved a useful source of reference. Other information came from internal circulars, letters, publicity and telephone directories in my collection.

Sadly Barbara Carter, always the most enthusiastic contributor to this book, died unexpectedly on the day it went to the publisher.

I

EXPENDITURE IN THE 1930S

Swindon had always known the importance of bookkeeping and by the early years of the twentieth century had realised the value of accounting for all its business transactions. The accounts of the CME Dept remained, in practice, separate from the other departments, all of whom came directly under the chief accountant at Paddington. Inevitably this independence was eroded somewhat after 1948.

The Chief Mechanical Engineers Department was a large department with a large budget. In the mid-1930s the annual turnover was about £14.5 million. Unlike other departments, they did not generate much revenue themselves. The money came from: 1) Revenue – money raised by the company through its business operation; and 2) Capital – money raised by the issue of shares and stocks or by loans and debenture stocks. In 1929 the assistant chief accountant gave a lecture to the Swindon Engineering Society, breaking down expenditure into four main categories. The single most expensive category was labour (wages claimed about 45 per cent of the budget), followed by materials, work bought in, coal, gas, water, electricity and tax. The CME Dept had been responsible for the purchase of all the company's coal and coke direct from the collieries, and that accounted for as much as 18 per cent of the budget. Some of the cost of coal, as well as its movement, was recovered from other departments, but the bulk went into locomotives and was charged to the Running Department of the CME, not to the Traffic Department. Coal was quickly being overtaken by electric for other forms of power, although a large amount continued to be used at the railway's gasworks. The CME's electrical assistant was responsible for the purchase of electricity for the whole company. The factory had produced its own electricity, but on requiring a new plant in the 1930s decided to receive it from the municipal supply. The Swindon Corporation's electrical power station at Moredon was completed about 1928–29 and had supplied some of the railway factory from the start.

The costs of new works, such as buildings and improved facilities, as well as machinery and plant renewal where there was a large initial outlay, came from the capital account. This was paid by head office, which would recover the money from the CME Dept over the anticipated life of that purchase, thus avoiding fluctuations in their budget by spreading the costs. Both revenue and capital accounts were used to protect the considerable assets of the CME Dept against depreciation – revenue for repair and maintenance and capital for replacement, like for like. The manufacture, repair and maintenance of rolling stock account for a significant proportion of the budget, so that only the additional costs of replacing the condemned stock was charged to capital. So as to improve and further standardise the range of locomotive types during the economic depression when expenditure was cut, suitable engines were classified as 'withdrawn' then rebuilt and outshopped as 'new', thus qualifying for capital funding. Some

One of the 100 large vacuum-braked vans built in the early 1930s for general merchandise. (*GWR Magazine*)

spending would, in the long term, save money. For instance, after another batch of King Class locomotives was completed, the *GWR Magazine* stated in 1930 that 'the building of large numbers of express locomotives has effected very considerable economies by 1) the haulage of longer and heavier trains (and presumably less of them) and 2) by reducing the number of banking engines needed'.

The allowance from revenue was cut each year from 1930 to 1933 and in 1932 the company was drawing on reserves. In his book *Swindon Steam 1921–1951*, Mr K.J. Cook said:

> In the late 1920s and 1930s when revenue was low, the renewal fund (Capital) was in a very healthy condition and with prices stable at that time it gave us considerable assistance in meeting our commitments ... during slump periods we had our normal allocation of money for machine tool renewal ...

As this money was only on loan to the CME Dept, the company must have been fairly sure the economy would soon improve. After 1933 the financial situation of the department did steadily improve, in line with an upturn in business on the railway, although there was an unexpectedly bad year in 1938. Large-scale dismissals were anounced on Friday 20 May that year, due to falling receipts for merchandise and coal movement. Authority from the board of directors had to be sought via the chief mechanical engineer for all projects where cost exceeded £100. The board therefore had to sanction all construction, reconstruction, alterations and improvements to rolling stock, but not the costs of ordinary repairs. Each British railway company was required to submit a statement to the Railway Rate Tribunal when it was set up in the early 1920s, showing all repair expenses for one year. From this information the figure for each company, known as Repairs Quantum, became their limit of expenditure and was adjusted each year by variations in the workload, wages and materials costs.

Supplies were purchased from, and manufactured items sold to, the Stores Department (at cost). Around 25 per cent of the budget was tied up, with work done and services rendered through contracts between departments and outside firms. The maintenance of stationary engines, cranes, and hoists at Stations was charged to the Traffic Department

19C – the carriage lifting shop in the 1930s. (*GWR Magazine*)

and likewise work done at docks, harbours and wharves was charged to the Docks Department. The drawing office did a lot of work for the Chief Civil Engineers (CCE) Department and the workshops made parts for the Permanent Way, and again this work was charged to them. Locomotive power, supplied for use with engineers' trains, was debited by the CME Dept, as was ashes from boilers which the CCE used as hardcore and to build up land. The Chief Mechanical Engineer's Department was totally separate in its role from the Engineering Department, as the CCE Dept was also known – the latter was responsible for fixed structures, such as buildings, bridges, platforms, turntable bases, lighting, canals, weighbridges, Permanent Way and the company's land. There was often close co-operation between these two departments. Their staff were, in many cases, subject to the same working instructions and conditions. The CME Dept could carry out civil engineer work on its own buildings with authority from the divisional engineer, then charge them for it.

There was a statutory requirement on the GWR to keep financial and statistical accounts under the railway companies (Accounts and Returns) Act of 1911, and that they be made up in prescribed form annually to 31 December. Thomas Minchin, an accounts clerk at Swindon Works, presented a paper to the Swindon Engineering Society in 1921 entitled Cost Accounting. In it, he attempted to explain that 'an accurate determination of costs is directly related to manufacturing efficiency' – an idea that he implies was far from common practice at that time. 'Only now was the company realising the value of complete Accounting because without it, inefficiencies cannot be properly identified,' he said. Careful record and scrutiny was made of all receipts and expenditure incurred at Swindon and Outstation. They endorsed the paradox – for efficiency, no expense should be spared in accounting for every penny spent and earned. Mr Minchin, then a recent Brunel medallist at the London School of Economics, pointed out that the expense of running the costing system (the assistant chief accountant's rough estimate was between 1*d* and 2*d* for every pound expended) was easily offset by the economies made. This was little comfort to the estimators (known as 'guessers' by some of the workshop staff) in the cost offices who had to chase the reasons, when actual costs exceeded estimated costs.

Workers in one of the large carriage and wagon shops in the 1920s. (Author's collection)

The costs of each completed lot or order was divided up into materials, labour and establishment charges. Material costs were fairly easy to ascertain thanks to an organised system of storekeeping. Enough material had to be purchased to complete the job but not too much so as to lock up capitol funds. A turnover of two and a half times per annum was claimed by the loco stores for the 45,000 or so items kept there. Other costs attributable to materials were receiving, checking and storage and these considerations were the responsibility of the Stores Department. Labour costs were divided between productive and non-productive workers. The piecework accounts gave management an accurate assessment of productivity in the shops and outstation, and also kept productive workers best utilised. Labour costs could be increased by poor working conditions and the attitude of some foremen. There are two detailed accounts of life on the shop floor at Swindon. Both Alfred Williams and Hugh Freebury talk of injustices heaped onto some men by their overseer, who knew he was accountable to no one, even if production was affected. Workers not directly employed in producing the work were, on the other hand, very difficult to assess for efficiency. Could they be better employed to assist production? Would there be less output if there were fewer of them?

Establishment charges included power, plant, rates, rent, lighting, water, coal, office sundries and anything that could not be costed accurately to a particular job. With regard to the latter, the CME Accounts required vast amounts of stationery. The dramatic rise in the cost of paper in 1937 caused the company great concern. Mr Minchin listed non-productive grades of workers under establishment charges (better known now as running costs) rather than labour costs. If only for the purposes of cost accounting, progressmen, clerks, typists, messengers, WC attendants and cleaners found themselves in the same category as works' officials, their assistants and foreman. I wonder what the chairman of the Society, Mr Hawksworth, who was present, thought of that. To be fair to non-productive workers, particularly the lower grades, where they were inefficient it was more likely the fault of the system, a reluctance of those with influence to consider change and the same mentality, no doubt, that had previously ensured the product was as good as it could be without regard for cost or time.

At the GWR Debating Society in 1933, a speaker, himself a member of the CME Dept, said, on the subject of improving the efficiency of staff, 'I advocate raising both the standard of education necessary for entrance into the railway service and the advertising of vacancies … the encouragement of promotion from the bottom up'. On co-operative efficiency, he spoke of the danger of placing department before company as the first priority. The writer of this prize-winning essay made no mention of competitive salaries and wages in the presence of one of the board of directors, but then the great company did not need to buy loyalty.

The assistant works manager said of the extent of the Swindon accounts: 'one cannot argue against the necessity of such an elaborate accounts system'. It appears from studies, such as that undertaken by Mr Minchin, that Swindon was well ahead of its head office at Paddington, where, at that time, cost accounts were produced as overall sets of figures and worthless for evaluation. Presumably this situation had developed because the work undertaken was not sold outside. The general manager Mr F.J.C. Pole said in his memoirs that his chief accountant had insisted that the cost of producing divisional profit and loss accounts would be too enormous and too difficult and so was not taken up in his time (up to 1929). However, by now it was realised that it was no longer enough for the company to know it was making a profit based on comparing monthly variations in traffic and docks receipts or maintaining a healthy general balance sheet each year. They too needed to account for all costs because as they stood, the total costs for a given period offered no clue as to whether they were excessive, and if they were, where that excess was incurred. Like all shrewd business people, the directors of the company saw opportunities to be exploited during the most depressed years of the early 1930s. At the Annual General Meeting, the chairman said that economies made would continue when trade revived. Swindon, with its superior methods of costing, had not waited until events forced economies upon them.

2

The Economic Depression

Generally, job security on the railways was very good but in the workshops, especially among the last in, it was not necessarily a job for life in the 1930s. New production methods inevitably meant less labour, so men affected were moved to other work and the balance was corrected with natural wastage. But when the dividend was down the company had a policy of discharging workshop labour. Word then soon spread through the town when manufacturing orders were to be cut. This was usually the start of the Western in recession and the decade started with all the worrying indicators. In 1929–30 the depression in trade caused a reduction in receipts, particularly in goods traffic. The company reduced wagon maintenance and manufacture, as well as repairs to secondary and branch line rolling stock. Short-time working was introduced throughout the workshops from August 1930. This was at a time when the department was still trying to make up for setbacks caused by the prolonged stoppages at the collieries three years earlier. The programme to replace main line locomotives and rolling stock was, therefore, almost as ambitious as ever and at odds with the austerity of time. Of particular note were a set of 'super saloons' built to rival the luxury carriages of the Pullman Car Co. Plans for extending and rebuilding facilities did include financial assistance from the government as part of the scheme to relieve unemployment. During the period, the Works built a plant for disinfecting coaches (known to the men as the Bug House), a 70-ton replacement weighbridge was installed in the carriage works and a springsmith shop had been built. The chair foundry had been extended and a huge new carriage repair shop was completed on land, recently acquired from the council. By the early 1930s a large area at the west end of the site was brought into use. Thousands of tons of ash and soil had to be brought in by the CME Dept to build up the land there. A 'concentration yard' for scrapping redundant stock and a large timber-stacking yard with workshops and sidings was built there – later they stored spare boilers there too.

Swindon Works, as elsewhere in industry, paid the least to those who produced the work, for the very sound but unfair reason that it was these workers who could be replaced or recalled when things improved. Consequently, few clerical and supervisory staff were discharged and again Swindon was a good example of this injustice, a major reason for the resentment the men felt toward 'them upstairs'. The years 1929–34 were the worst, with unemployment nationally rising to 3.5 million or 15.6 per cent of the labour force. According to *GWR Magazine* there were 13,531 employed in the factory in 1931. Another source says the figure was just over 11,000 a year later (the lowest of the whole period). The majority of job losses across the department came from within the town, which had by then over 3,000 registered as workless (unemployed). The Swindon GWR Chargemens Association called a meeting to try to encourage those with local influence to help improve business for the railway company. They appealed to the local MP, to the townspeople via the press, to the Chamber of Commerce and to tradesmen to help divert back traffic that had been lost to road hauliers. The railway companies had become alarmed at the amount of public money being spent on the roads, which was well beyond that amounting from vehicle and petrol tax. The chargemen reasoned that the railway company provided their livelihoods; therefore they should all support them.

Beryl Wynn's (*née* Odey) father was a French polisher in the carriage works throughout the 1930s. She said, 'although our Dad always had full employment, Mother had to get all the groceries "on tick" every short week and pay up every balance week.' So it is difficult to imagine how railway families managed when the working week was cut to four or even three days and they could not fall back on assistance from relatives or from the government. It was not until 1946 that mothers could claim 'Family Allowance' for each child, excluding the eldest. For the poor souls whose 'services were no longer required', the dole queue was almost certainly the only alternative. The dole payout was subject to a means test, which meant an official would come to the house and assess the collateral; the family piano, the mantle clock and any other non-essentials would have to be sold before any money could be claimed. Casual work would be sought as well, to supplement the meagre dole allowance. If it was suspected that poverty was causing a deterioration of health, a person or family might receive handouts organised by the church or civic groups. The Mayor Mr William Robins, elected in 1932, was a clerk in the factory. He said one of the most beneficial schemes during his term was the borough council allocating allotment land to the unemployed. Later, when he worked in the stores order office, Mr Robins was the organising secretary of the Railway Clerks Association.

Unlike single women, men had little or no hope of alternative employment locally, a situation which allowed the company a long period of industrial harmony with its workers. The men received eight days' holiday annually, plus six Bank Holidays, which was all unpaid until 1938, adding to their predicament. Between 1930–33, the Mechanics' Institute lost a third of its paying members, but this seemed to make little difference to the numbers going away on 'Trip'. For those who still qualified it was almost no cheaper to stay home on 'Trip Day'. Beryl Wynn said her father never enjoyed 'Trip' because, like so many others, he was worried about the labour discharges that took place a few weeks later if the company was doing badly. The weeks following 'Trip holiday' were bound to be difficult for the manual worker if he and his family spent the whole week away. 'Adams', the pawn broker in Fleet Street, always did brisk trade at this time of year. A couple of local artists had their comical sketches of 'Trip' published as postcards earlier in the century. The theme was usually the financial predicament the holiday had caused. One showed the 'Annual Wash' on the eve. The journey was depicted as the 'Annual Rush' and the period following was the 'Annual Hush', showing the wife and kids behind the door when the rent collector or money lender called. These pathetic situations appeared comical because there was more than a little that working families could identify with. Now the effects of the Depression meant that the circumstances of their parents were back, if they had ever gone away. 'Waste not' and 'make do and mend' were sayings well known to Swindon people long before the war years.

It was the men in the shops who viewed impending retirement with anxiety and hoped they could find some sort of paying employment elsewhere when they reached sixty-five. If they were unwilling or unable to pay into something, like the 'Sick Fund Society', where a superannuation allowance was paid upon retirement, they would, assuming they lived that long, regret that decision. Some locals say their fathers and uncles suffered hardship in retirement even after the war, but subject to a medical check, some men could continue to work after sixty-five. Despite all this, factory workers' prospects were significantly better than those who worked in rural areas and Swindon suffered far less of the changing fortunes characteristic of other towns which were dominated by one employer.

Mr K.J. Cook says in his book *Swindon Steam* that 'Railway Accountancy is very strictly controlled by Acts of Parliament with the object of safeguarding the interests of rail users against monopolies'. The controls included wage levels which had been set after the First World War when the men's negotiating powers were still ineffective. In the 1930s the British economy was in no condition to introduce a minimum wage, as the Americans had done for their industrial workers and others in 1938, not least because of the cost of the knock-on effect up through the pay scales. Those living on the wage grades in the CME Dept did little more than 'get by' in the 1930s, and despite a steady fall of prices in the shops, workers without a trade were below the poverty line. Junior salaried staff were likely to see their pay increase over time, sufficient for them to provide for a wife and family, unlike the manual workers who had little or no scope to improve their living standards, unless they were still working into the 1950s when things did start to improve.

A mortgage required an income of between £150 and £200 a year, so the newly-wed shopman was confined to a two-up/two-down house in an Edwardian or Victorian terrace within site of the Works. Up until the mid-1930s, his rent would be between 6 and 7s a week, or between 12 and 20 per cent of his net wages, depending on his trade – and he was responsible for the upkeep of the dwelling and for all general repairs. Homes around the town centre were getting a bit dilapidated by the early 1930s. Jack Fleetwood said:

> ... nobody had a bathroom, we brought in the galvanised tin bath that hung up in the back yard, nor did anyone have a flushing toilet. There was a gap in the wall of our lean-to kitchen extension, when dad had finished with the evening paper it was pushed through to our neighbours.

The better paid could, if they wished, buy a house a little further out. Areas to the north and east of the town were being developed; a semi-detached house on the northern road development cost £365 and a detached one was £400. Overall, the borough's figures were quite impressive – 19,000 Swindon dwellings were owner occupied in 1939.

In the early 1930s, building societies were making much of the fact that houses were cheaper than ever, due to low interest rates and cheaper material costs, but the financial crisis in the economy meant lending was severely limited. The GWR could arrange loans for house purchase, offering terms more favourable than the building societies. Their savings bank required a repayment per month, sufficient only to cover the interest accrued and any amount beyond that was optional. They also had a working arrangement with the Swindon Permanent Building Society, offering slightly more favourable terms for railwaymen. The workforce in the factory were generally less likely to be transferred away and therefore better placed to take up a mortgage. The loans were directed at the staff grades, not only because they were best able to repay, but also their employment with the company was more secure. Upon being married, both Jack and George Petfield moved out to the council estate built between the wars at Pinehurst. The rent in 1938 was 13s a week. The Old Town ('up Nob Hill') was of varying affluence, but very few wage grades lived up there, unless the previous generation had purchased the house. Here, one could rub shoulders with the managers. One street in Old Town – known as Bloater Avenue – was said, according to the detractors from New Swindon, to have such expensive houses that the occupiers could afford only bloaters for their tea. Jack found out that the bloater principle did exist when he worked with a bloke known as 'Granny'. Granny was a moulder in the brass foundry and ate nothing but bread and jam. Whenever he was questioned about his diet he would steer the conversation around to his house which 'is in Goddard Avenue'. After the war, it was possible for shopmen, of no additional means, to purchase homes of their own even though prices had gone up considerably. 'Bert Allen, one of our chargehands, was even more frugal than Granny,' said Jack, although he lived in a more modest place near Cambria Bridge. Jack said:

> Bert was obsessive about economising but he was no miser, he offered me an interest-free loan if I wanted to buy a house when I got married in 1945. People were far more neighbourly in those days and especially willing to help newly-weds, but repaying money was a big responsibility and I declined the offer.

Ariel views of the Works were very popular in the 1920s and '30s. Although they were effective in showing the vastness of the site, few showed more than about a third of it. (Author's collection)

The only extravagance for many men of the Works might be to see Swindon Town's home matches; railwaymen made up a good proportion of Town supporters and occasionally the Works closed early for a big game. This happened only once in the 1930s, in January 1938, when the factory closed at midday for an important cup match that evening. Beer was about 4*d* a pint before the war – Best Bitter maybe 6*d* – less in the many workingmen's clubs. There were plenty of watering holes close by the factory and they were never empty. Jack had heard of the reputation of some, even as a child. In the railway estate, the Cricketers Arms had a spirit licence but the rest were just beerhouses. Until about 1936, children could go into public houses (but not the workingmen's clubs) and collect beer for their parents in jugs and bottles. While some spent more than they could afford on drink, when their family went without, many dutiful family men abstained. A few didn't drink for religious reasons or because they lived in fear of their wives, but most men took their responsibilities seriously. They had become conditioned to a life of thrift long before taking on a family; they were more likely to be found on their allotment, thus supplementing the family budget in their spare time. A familiar sight around the town were the allotment fences made up of old railway enamel signs. When railway equipment was replaced it was sent to Swindon Works for disposal and the men could buy such items for a small charge. Enamel signs, and later steel coach panels, were very durable and kept the rabbits away from the vegetables. Jack Fleetwood said:

> A lot of families kept chickens or rabbits but when came the time to kill them they would often ask me to do it. Catching rabbits was a popular pastime but the ones in the Concentration Yard at the back of the works were left alone and consequently it became overrun, it wasn't that the company objected to rabbit traps, but living on a diet of mainly wood, they were inedible.

Rabbits could be bought from a man called 'Cockle Jack' who came round selling them from a pony and cart. They were a bit cheaper than those in the shops, at about a shilling each, and

Newsagent Joe Sheppard on his Sunday morning round in Bathampton Street, in the late 1920s or early '30s. (B. Harber)

the skin could be sold to the 'rag and bone man' for 3*d*. Horse meat was available as a cheap alternative meal during wartime, if not before, and some people ate pigeon meat.

The GWR employee, if he or she was the main supporter of the family, could take advantage of cheap coal (minimum 2cwt) or scrap timber from the company, delivered to the door by a private haulier using a horse and cart. Wood delivery drivers often had a deformity or infirmity and could not pass the medical test to go 'inside', or they may have had to leave because of a disability. Some enterprising retired workers made themselves a handcart and put a sticker in their front window advertising 'Factory Wood Delivered'. In the 1930s wood tickets cost you 1*s* per cwt, and a little more if you required delivery to one of the surrounding villages. By the 1950s it was half a crown and the coal a little more of course. In the Second World War the supply of cheap household coal was stopped because of alternative demands being made on ships and trains that carried it. Workers and their families then had to burn wood to heat their homes.

Timber could be collected from the wood wharf by Whitehouse Bridges, thus saving the small hauliers' fee. Like all second-hand materials, the wood was classified as either scrap or serviceable. The official view was 'care should be taken that timber disposed of as firewood is such as could not be used with advantage for Company's purposes'. In 1947 the railway's own transport took over the deliveries of coal and timber. This must have been hard on the people who had made a few coppers from those customers. Other useful scrap could be purchased, such as old flue tubes from locomotive boilers, at a shilling each. Jack said that sometimes after paying you could swap them and take out new ones. Three of these tubes fixed together made a sturdy washing line, although when it was available signal rodding was preferred, as it didn't rust so quickly.

By 1938 the country was slowly recovering from the recession and there was work available for semi-skilled and skilled men. It was, therefore, a shock when about twenty-four men on the 'loco side' were under notice to go, and some short-time working was introduced in March due to building programmes being completed. There were threats of further cuts and by July well over a thousand were to go.

3
PAY AND NEGOTIATIONS

Standard salaries, wages and hours of duty had all been established at Railway Rate Tribunals set up under the Railways Act of 1921, and became known as 'national agreements'. The agreements were based partly on the ordinary annual expenditure figures set by the Tribunal for each of the four railway companies. Tribunals set up to deal primarily with railwaymen's pay would be supplied with verbal and written evidence from both sides. The unions' representatives would argue that their members and their families suffered unreasonable hardship, and even ill health, and deserved a better share of the profits, a shorter working week and paid holidays. For the Management Negotiating Committee, the Great Western's chief accountant Mr Cope, among others, would present the statistics for the annual expenditure and revenue and argue a case for moderation. Separate agreements for the CME workers, such as footplatemen, supervisory staff, clerical staff, women and girl clerks and conciliation staff, but excluding the shopmen, were worked out, and all subsequent questions concerning pay would have to come within the scope of these agreements.

Subsequent pay adjustments had to be agreed by the Central Wages Board or, on appeal, by the National Wages Board, bodies set up by the joint railway companies consisting of a panel of representatives from both sides. The wages boards became increasingly unpopular with both unions and management. The problem was the constitution of the boards, which were expected to sit as judges and remain impartial, and as a result negotiations became slow and laborious. In particular, the deadlock over the need to further reduce earnings in 1932–33 showed the shortcomings of settling these matters through the wages boards. The railways suggested that the machinery at the local level might be the way to determine questions relating to pay rates in the future, so in early 1934 the machinery, as established under the Railway Act of 1921, was terminated.

A new Machinery of Negotiation emerged to cover major issues of standard salaries, wages and hours of duty through 'discussion or negotiation' – the former terms 'conciliation and arbitration' were now omitted from the dialogue. Before any question could be dealt with under the machinery, it had to be first referred to the railway company concerned through the appropriate channels. The improved means of communications offered did not mean the company had gone soft. They instructed their officials to scrutinise 'the book' carefully before conceding to proposals or alleged injustices. The memorandum now included a detailed disciplinary procedure, although there was no provision for negotiations over disciplinary or management matters. The stance towards those accused of serious misconduct was also retained, despite union insistence of a proper hearing. The company rule book of 1937 stated that anyone guilty of misconduct and dismissed 'forfeits any right to wages for any period subsequent to the completed week preceding his dismissal or suspension prior to dismissal'.

Any question within the scope of the new local machinery, but not resolved, could be referred to the headquarters of the trade union concerned and they could raise the matter at a higher level or go directly to the general manager Mr (later Sir) James Milne. Agreements reached and minuted through the various machinery channels became operational from the beginning of the next complete paybill period or from such a date settled for the purpose. If the matter was still not resolved, the parties could go to arbitration through the Railway Staff Tribunal (formally the Industrial Court) for decision.

Shopmen made up almost 50 per cent of the CME Dept and the rest were divided between the (Civil) Engineers, Docks Department and the Signal Works. Railway shopmen could be engineers, coach builders or construction workers and had been paid at rates set for each craft and governed by the fortunes prevailing in those industries. District rates, as they were known, were not related to other manual railway workers' rates. They did, as the name implies, vary, depending on local conditions.

At the shopmen's industrial court hearing of 1922 both the railway companies and the National Union of Railwaymen (NUR) were keen to bring their shop workers' rates in line with other railway workers, as had happened so successfully during the First World War, but they disagreed about how future increases in the rates should be negotiated. The NUR wanted pay rates as decided by the court to be subject to the sliding scale, the way it was for the

Opposite: Fixing plywood roofs to 12-ton wagons; eight roofs were completed per gang, per day. Note the suspended cradle for tools. (BR National Railway Museum)

Right: With the work suspended from a swinging jib, hot riveting was done using a Fielding and Platt hydraulic fixed riveter. (BR National Railway Museum)

conciliation grades. The railway companies' view was that the rates, fixed on the principles set by them, should vary with the national variations of the engineering trade. The Amalgamated Engineering Union (AEU), and other craft unions which still represented many of the railway shopmen, naturally wanted things to stay as they were. The court would not come down on one side or the other but recommended the establishment of local machinery to incorporate pay issues. The GWR had begun to offer facilities for the establishment of shop and piecework committees in the same month that they were making their representations to the court, within weeks of Mr Collett becoming chief mechanical engineer. Swindon men received a circular in February 1922, offering the option of local committees if the majority of men in each area wanted it. They would be made up of shop stewards and representatives of all grades, irrespective of membership of a particular union. Matters of piecework, welfare, discipline and improving working methods were within the scope of the new machinery, but not pay. The management saw the committees as a way of 'securing good mutual understanding with the men'. There was even an appeal committee if matters could not be settled, but not all areas initially took up the idea – some saw it as undermining the union process.

By the late 1920s, following the general strike, a worsening economic situation and increasing competition from road transport, all sides were looking for the opportunity to present their case and receive a fully considered response, and not to repeat the confrontations

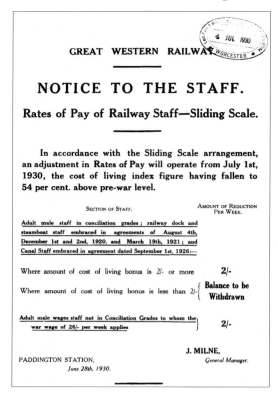

(Author's collection)

of the past. The railway companies, no doubt with government backing, extended negotiating powers of the shopmen's committees in 1927 and the GWR issued a hardcover booklet to each man summarising the scheme. Only now, five years after it was recommended by the industrial court, did the negotiating machinery allow for questions, not only of pay but of pay rates.

Throughout the period, the employer expressed wages in shillings and pence – for those too young to remember, 20s was equal to £1. I see no point in giving the present equivalent monetary figures to earnings, nor do I attempt to compare the working man's lot over the intervening fifty to seventy-five years. I have included a section about the home lives of former railway families. Their circumstances speak for themselves. Rates of pay referred to the weekly (not hourly) amount payable, excluding any bonuses or allowances. The enginemen and firemen had long since standardised rates of pay throughout the company, unlike the shopmen, where every type of trade had attracted a different rate for the job. This was due to separately negotiated agreements which had been worked out locally and became known as district rates. The 1922 industrial court hearing for railway shopmen achieved a degree of 'uniformity and order in a vast and complex system'. The various trades, with one or two exceptions, were grouped together into eight pay bands, with the variation between the highest and lowest pay being reduced. Seven shillings of the war wage bonus was transferred to the basic rate as a result of the 1922 reforms.

In the late 1930s when it became more commonly known as the cost-of-living allowance, the bonus paid was 16s 6d for all skilled, semi-skilled and labourers in the shops. Shopmen were graded according to their experience and what type of work they were put on. A Grade 1 man could be paid up to 8s more than the man next to him. Workshop men in industrial towns and cities, including Swindon, were paid more than men in smaller towns and rural areas because of the living costs. Workers in the London area got a little more again. A patternmaker was paid more than a fitter or skilled turner (lathe operator). A toolmaker was highly skilled and respected but his rate did not reflect this. Much of the metalwork done on mills, slotters, planers, shapers, borers, grinders, drills, capstan and turret lathes was simple and repetitive and required only limited skill. At that time the metal machinists were classed as skilled, although that skill was acquired with experience and little formal training. Because of this, these grades were easier to replace than the journeyman and the company could pay them less. The time-served turner, for instance, undertook specialised work and was paid more than those who just machined loco or carriage wheels and axles. A first-year apprentice received 14*s* a week, which included a war wage of 4*s*. Out of that, he may have a sizable deduction to repay his training fees and the loan that paid for his tools. If he was living at home with his parents, he would be expected to hand over the remainder to mother for bed and board. As he approached his twenty-first birthday, and possibly a letter stating 'his services were no longer required', he would be getting 28*s*, which included 8*s* war wage. As is well known, many ex-apprentices later returned and could expect a journeymen's rate of between 38 to 48*s*, depending on age, experience and the type of work undertaken. Adult pay rates started at the age of twenty – apprentices excluded, this had gone up from eighteen years in the early 1920s.

Of the skilled shopmen of the 1930s and early '40s, in 'Area 1', which included Swindon, most were eligible for the 46*s* rate. This included coach body makers, loco erectors, cabinet makers, fitters and electricians. Some carriage and wagon department trades, such as wheelwrights, painters, wagon riveters and coach trimmers, were regarded less highly and were paid less. Peter Reade said his first pay when learning to be a blacksmith was 30*s*. This was the starting figure for a smiths striker. After three years learning the trade, he would be eligible for 38 to 46*s*, the maximum for most journeymen at that time. Most of the semi-skilled rates were between 30 and 36*s*. If the work was heavy, such as boilermaking, or if working with hot metals, as did the stamper and drop hammerman, the wages were equal to those of many skilled grades. A semi-skilled Grade 1 wagon builder or springmaker's rate was also equal to that of the lower end of the skilled man's pay range. When starting new work, materials, nuts, washers and split pins had to be drawn from the stores, and tools were issued from a tool store. Two grades worked in the shop stores, the 'stores issuer' and the 'storesman'. The issuer was in charge and the storesman was his general assistant. Their wages were worked out as a percentage above that of the Grade 2 labourer in the same area. The rate for the stores issuer was between 29 and 44*s*. Depending on his grade, the storesman received between 27 and 31*s*.

School leavers did not go straight 'inside' at fourteen years old, so Jack Fleetwood started work as an errand boy at the Wiltshire Bacon Company shop in Regent Street, Swindon, next to the new Savoy Cinema.

> After a twelve month (period) I went into the works, starting in the 'R' shop 'scraggery', machining the end faces on nuts (other railway works across the country put boys on very similar work at first). For this I got 12*s* 6*d* on the short week and 18*s* to £1 for the balance (piecework payout) week.

This was 1937. Previously, piecework bonus was not paid until the person reached the age of eighteen, although their work was taken into account. Jack knew the foundry labourers at Swindon as 'the 31 shilling men', the semi-skilled were 'the 39 shilling men', and by the start of the war a semi-skilled iron moulder was 'a 47 shilling man'. The brass moulder took home slightly less.

Most men in the workshops rarely had the chance of ' Sunday Time', which was time-and-a-half of flat rate, but they did get to work nights, thereby claiming the higher rate of time-and-a-quarter from 10 p.m. to 6 a.m. At Swindon, and possibly elsewhere, with

A male worker rivets
a locomotive firebox
while a female worker
feeds in hot rivets as
required. (BR National
Railway Museum)

the gradual introduction of the more reliable electric machinery, a fitter would be paid to be on-call at home at night, with someone being sent out to knock him up if required. Promotion to chargeman or inspector was considered an honour and was a good move towards becoming the foreman, but otherwise the small increase in pay did not tempt everyone to take on the extra responsibility. Promotion to foreman increased a man's income considerably and enabled him the opportunity to progress up through a lengthy seniority scale and the salary increases that went with it. All the company's supervisory staff, including the CME Dept foremen, had the same salary scale which was made up of five classes. Clerical staff were also on the same scale, excluding the lower half of their Class 5. The foremen were paid their salary in weekly parts. A junior foreman was paid between 65d and 81s, depending on the number of men he had under his control and the length of time in that position. At the top end, the chief foreman, the man in overall charge of several areas and large numbers of men, would receive between 120 and 130s, more than double that of the tradesman or staff Grade 4 under his control.

Of the grades not directly employed in, but allied to workshops, the staff at railway electrical generating stations were paid enhanced rates. The electrical power house at Swindon supplying its workshops, however, was not considered (by the industrial court in 1922) to be of sufficient capacity and the skilled workers therein were paid rates set for ordinary electricians. The plant closed in favour of the municipal supply in the 1930s. The dozen or so works fire brigade staff

Looking down the main shopping street in the town – Regent Street. The Wiltshire Bacon Company on the right was where Jack Fleetwood worked until he went into Swindon Works. (Author's collection)

received 58s at ordinary grade, plus of course an on-call allowance. Gatemen and watchmen were paid according to local conditions. Although classed as semi-skilled, they were paid no more than a labourer, with a minimum of 30s.

In the offices male workers up to the age of eighteen were officially referred to as 'junior clerks' and female workers were 'girl clerks'. At Swindon they were known collectively as 'office juniors'. They did little clerical work and plenty of errand running and odd jobs. In the mid-1930s, boys could start a year earlier than girls, at fifteen years old, on a salary of £35 per annum. Girls began their clerical careers with a wage of 17s 6d per week. Possibly unique among railway grades, this was equal to the annual salary of their male counterpart of the same age. The rates of pay for male and female clerks had been set at the national agreements for clerical staffs in 1920. The lowest ranked clerks started at Grade (or Class) 5 upon reaching eighteen years of age. Women started on a Grade 2, and although now paid less, this was the equivalent to a male Grade 5. The rates of pay for male clerical staff, published periodically by the NUR and the Railway Clerks Association, show that in 1937 a junior clerk received an annual salary of £80. This had risen to £192, or 10s, by 1948. There was a £10 annual increment following each birthday to a maximum salary of £200, although they should have been promoted into a higher class before reaching this limit. Mr F.G. Richens of the CME Dept said, in a lecture he gave to the GWR Debating Society in 1934, 'the automatic wage advancements up to the age of 31 make no distinction between the keen and the apethetic employee'. Women clerks, or 'W1's to give them their proper name, were paid weekly and started on 30s. At the other end, the Class 1 female clerk received a maximum of 70s per week in 1937.

The course of progress up through the grades depended on age, experience and qualifications. Promotion was usually from within the department, if not the office. George Petfield says he does not remember anyone coming in from outside to fill a more senior position, not until the 1960s anyway. Grades 5 to 1 excluded ancillary office staff, employed entirely as timekeepers, messengers, assistants and those who supplied information to the clerks making out paybills.

At the top of the pay scale, the senior males (apart from those reaching the 'special classes') in Class 1, with a minimum of five years in that post, were awarded £335 to £350 in 1937 and £460 to £490 in 1948 – the higher figure was discretional. Beyond Grade 1, promotion to 'Special A' up to 'C' was as high as the most ambitious person could normally hope to reach before retirement. The salary for 'Special C' was about £500 per annum in the mid-1930s, with a little more after two years of service. This had risen to a starting figure of £600 in 1948. Staff were privileged to holidays with pay well before the shop workers. They also received their money in full from the company for a limited period when out sick. Staff Grades 2 to 5 got twelve days, plus Good Friday and Christmas Day, but not until they had a minimum of ten years of service. Those in Classes 1 and 2 got fifteen days, and those in 'special classes' received eighteen days' paid holidays. As well as the concessionary rail travel awarded to all workers, senior clerical and supervisory staff got first-class rail passes when they had completed two years of service.

In 1939 there were increases in the minimum wages of conciliation workers to 47s for men and 36s 6d for women. From 1 January 1940, it was agreed with the three rail unions to make a war wage advance of 4s per week to adult male conciliation grades or £10 per annum to male salaried staff, and 3s per week to adult females on the staff. Peter Reade joined the company in 1939 working in the smith's shop. He was sixteen years old and so received the standard rate for juniors of that age which was 10s, plus a small percentage war bonus amounting to about another 5 per cent. The war wage bonus was introduced in 1915 and was retained in principal (and name!) throughout the inter-war years and on into the next war. This cost-of-living allowance amounted to 10 to 15 per cent extra (the higher percentage given to the lower paid) after the first twelve months of war. It was funded by the government and continued to be reviewed twice yearly – the rate of increase required to keep pace with the cost of living accelerated as the war continued.

The 1940s, despite all the upheaval, were to be more lucrative and secure for the men (and women) not called up. Now the amount of extra time required at the workplace was excessive, with twelve-hour day or night shifts for six days of the week, and even the option of working the Sunday as well, but as the workers started to show signs of fatigue it became counterproductive and a limit was imposed. Despite the increasing cost of living and rates of Income Tax, the extra work allowed the workers a degree of financial freedom. There were only the basic items available in the shops, but for those used to struggling to make ends meet, these were better times. The rationing of consumables started at the beginning of 1940 but there had already been shortages. Bread, cigarettes and beer never went on 'ration', but shopkeepers kept their limited supplies aside for their regulars. In the middle of 1941 it became necessary to ration clothing and the following year it was sweets. Barbara Carter remembers running down Milton Road towards 'the factory' because she was always late. She said:

> At the bottom opposite the Medical Centre if you saw a queue of people which disappeared round the corner into Faringdon Road, that could only mean one thing, Blackwell's sweetshop actually had sweets for sale. For some workers the temptation was too much and they arrived late clutching a bag of wartime sweets.

John Brettell started his career as an office boy in 1941 and received the usual 8s a week. 'Although I was down as working in "D" shop I actually spent my time in the Newburn Carriage Sheds,' he said. The Royal Engineers had taken over most of this building, which was only two years old. The railway staff that were there came over from 'D1' and 'D2' shops. When John started his apprenticeship on his sixteenth birthday, he too got the 10s rate but the bonus had by then, two years into the war, gone up to 65 per cent. Years later he managed to get a copy of his personal record card when the staff records were all being relocated. This shows precisely how an apprentice fitter and turner were paid in wartime and how the war

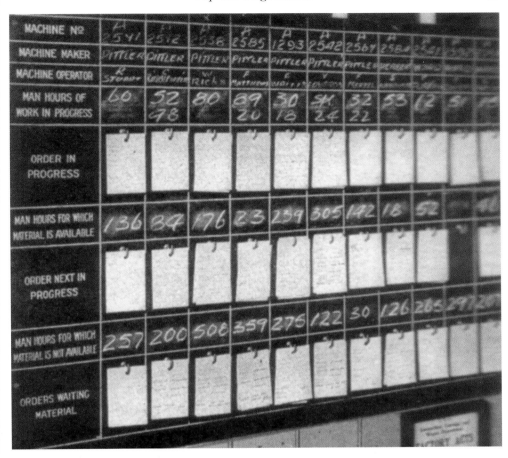

Loading Board in 'T' shop office showing machine work in hand. Note the Factories Act notice below. (BR National Railway Museum)

wage almost reached 100 per cent. At each birthday, the wages increased: in 1942, 11s 6d plus 7s; 1943, 14s plus 8s 10d; 1944, 19s 6d plus 17s 2d; 1945, 23s plus 21s 9d.

In 1942 the trade unions submitted pay claims for minimum rated conciliation and salaried staffs. As usual, the workers representatives, the unions and the national shopmen's and electrical councils put in for more than they would settle for. The *GWR Magazine* reported that with effect from 9 March, the 'Railway Staff National Tribunal' would grant the following: the total war wage to be increased to 4s 6d per week for adult male conciliation grades who earn the minimum 48s industrial rate. Adult females (aged twenty and over) taking the place of men received the same rates and increases as the minimum rated men. Class 5 male clerical staff were to be extended one extra annual increment of £10 to a maximum of £210 per annum at the age of thirty-two years. The Class 4 maximum would not exceed £220. The Class 2 female increment would rise to 2s 6d per week to a maximum of 62s 6d at thirty-two years of age. And of all the increases, only the salaried staff increases were guaranteed until the war's end. The tribunal left it to the two sides to consider the effects of this upon the pay differentials of the higher grades.

Within days of the end of the war, and with the backing of the new Labour government, agreement was reached between the Railway Executive and the unions for improvements in standard rates of pay for all grades, an increase in the war advance, concessions in respect of annual leave and the Sunday rate increased to time-and-three-quarters. The unions claim for a forty-four-hour working week was resisted, but only until June 1947 when most CME grades would work five eight-hour shifts and a four-hour Saturday morning per week. Office cleaners who had worked forty-four hours or more per week before 1947 were paid 1s 6½d per hour, plus an extra 7s 6d by the Court of Enquiry pay review of June 1947. The one week or six days paid annual leave entitlement for all wages staff was to be doubled from 1946. This was, as before, still subject to completing twelve months of service. In addition, all grades already received days off with ordinary rate pay for working Whit Monday or August bank holiday. In 1947 the salaried staff's ordinary rostered working hours were reduced from forty-eight to forty-two per week, to be worked as five long and one short turns, or six equal turns over six days. Those in Classes 2 to 6, the special classes, and female Class 1 were to be granted fifteen weekdays' annual leave instead of the twelve previous, although this was still subject to completing ten years of service first. Jack Fleetwood became a junior foreman in 1945. His first wage on the staff was £6 per week. The journeyman's rate in the late 1940s was on average £5 to £6, an increase of at least 110 per cent in ten years, just keeping pace with the cost of living.

By 1948 pay scales for female clerks started at 66s 6d up to a maximum of 112s. The Class 1 male clerk received nearly double the female figure – perhaps his ranking was considered more equal than hers! The ladies got twelve weekdays' holiday and in common with all staff, they now only had to be in post just twelve months to qualify. Rates for railway clerks in 1948 remained the same until the early 1950s. Equal pay for women in the offices did not happen until as late as 1964 with the introduction of the Sex Discrimination Act. Wages grade clerks, formerly 'unappointed clerks', received a weekly wage equivalent to salaried clerks when they were in permanent positions and when their work was commensurate in importance.

War bonus's were replaced by higher basic rates and rates for British railway conciliation grades started at 96s for most unskilled male grades by 1950. Beyond that, the pay scales continued to be complex, despite the 'reorganisation' of 1948, with neither side willing to make the concessions that streamlining the rates would require. The trade unions published booklets detailing the different rates of pay for conciliation, shopmen and salaried staff. They also gave overtime rates, lodging allowances and annual leave entitlement, as well as time off to attend a funeral, rest intervals between turns of duty, demotion and redundancy. Junior conciliation grades started at 39s per week for fifteen year olds, up to 66s for nineteen-year olds. Women were paid 2s less through the same scale. If a junior did the work of an adult for more than four hours of the turn of duty, they were to be paid the adult rate for that turn.

In February 1951 an agreement between the Railway Executive and the three main rail trade unions gave all conciliation and salaried staff a further increase, broadly equivalent to 7.5 per cent above previous rates. The new British Railway's management said in the declaration issued to every employee that 'only part of the extra £12 million to be spent on salaries and wages can be recovered from savings effected under nationalisation, this means that in order to find the money passengers and senders of goods by rail will be asked to pay more'. The executives were keen to give the impression of good relations with the unions, hoping to strengthen trust and maintain labour relations. However, as a consequence of the pay increases, 'opportunities of reorganisation and technical progress must be given full scope'. In this context, that statement could only mean reducing unprofitable services and job losses, the beginnings of what became the Modernisation Plan of 1955. All pay increases offered by the British Transport Commission now included conditions of increased productivity, which the unions would resist.

Harry Bartlett moved from fitter and turner in '15 shop' to the cost office, also on the carriage side, in 1957. By this time orders for carriages were being diverted elsewhere, causing a surplus of labour on the carriage side. Harry started on 233s as a temporary estimator. As a

INCOME TAX YEAR 1944-45

CERTIFICATE OF PAY AND TAX DEDUCTED

Fleetwood J

CHECK No 6148

(Name of employee and Works No., if any)

Code No. at 5 April, 1945
(Enter " E " if an Emergency Card
is in use at 5 April, 1945)   *14*

District
Refce. (if any) *6537/763*

	Gross pay			Tax		
	£	s.	d.	£	s.	d.
1. Pay and tax in respect of previous employment(s) in 1944-45 taken into account in arriving at the tax deductions made by me/us						
2. PAY AND TAX IN MY/OUR EMPLOYMENT ...	*344*	*4*	*2*	*76*	*18*	*0*

I/We certify that the particulars given above include the total amount of pay (including overtime, bonus, commission, etc.) paid to you by me/us in the year ended 5 April, 1945 and the total tax deducted by me/us (less any refunds) in that year.

....Employer

....Date

TO THE EMPLOYEE. Keep this certificate. It will help you to check the Notice of Assessment which the Tax Office will send you in due course.

P60

£5-13-0 AFTER TAX

'Jack' Fleetwood's 'P60' certificate for the year ended 5 April 1945. (J. Fleetwood)

journeyman he got slightly more but now he was on the staff and could climb the new pay scale with annual increments.

There is no mention of the 'special classes' in the NUR (National Union of Railwaymen) pay rates for salaried staff before nationalisation. So it is likely that this was the start of lower management in the GWR and anyone promoted above Grade 1 was presumably expected to sever all union loyalties. Only senior management were above a 'Special C' grade and only they were not paid in cash. They would receive an annual salary by way of a bank cheque sent down from Paddington with a representative of the chief clerk. Alan Peck noted in his rough book while working in the drawing office that the vacant post of outstation materials assistant to the loco works manager was being offered with a starting salary of £650. This was in 1949 and presumably this position, which interested the twenty-nine-year-old Mr Peck, was then the minimum starting figure for senior staff – later, as archivist for the Western Region, Mr Peck wrote a history of Swindon Works. The CME's chief accountant Mr Gardner said in his lecture to the Swindon Engineering Society in 1929 that 'the salaries figure is of course subject to constant scrutiny in that additional staff are only appointed after careful consideration and advances (increases) in salary are only made as authorised by the Board of Directors'. Established management positions were rarely, if ever, considered dispensable on the Great Western but there could be questions asked about increases in personal expenses or why certain sections of a department had increased its manpower.

The GWR introduced piecework about 1910. They were not among the first railway companies to offer financial bonuses or profit sharing to improve output, even though it was shown to work. Manual workers in the CME Dept were either on piecework or day work, or sometimes a combination of the two. Men on piecework were paid a bonus, calculated as a percentage of their daily wage rate and paid out once a fortnight – converting the piecework figures on to the paybills fortnightly instead of every week greatly reduced the pressure on the accounts department. The percentage received depended on the productivity averaged out over the week, between all the gangs working in sections within the shop or outstation. A man could expect a fairly consistent weekly bonus, known as 'the balance', as long as the work was not held up before reaching his gang. Every job in the CME Dept had

Dinner break in 'R' machine shop in 1924. As with most workshops, the machine shop still required men working at benches using hand tools. (R. Hatherall, courtesy of R. Clarke)

to be priced at every stage (or detail). Piece prices were set to allow the worker not less than 33.3 per cent of his basic day or time rate. This figure had been more generous than other railway companies, until the industrial court ruling of July 1922. The balance represented the amount by which the total value of the piecework certificate exceeded the base rate earnings of the gang during a particular fortnight. In the workshops, the shop clerks issued the stores order forms and drawings with each batch of work to be undertaken. The inspector, a staff Grade 2, was responsible for checking the standard of work produced and completion of the order. Tables showing the various rates were held by the chargeman of the gang, and each stage was expressed either as a price or, if the job was repetitive, as time allowed. Some jobs required teamwork to complete, as in Peter Reade's case. It was he, as the blacksmith, who earned the bonus for his strikers and himself, as they could only work at his speed. The blacksmiths were exceptional in that they would work out from the drawing how much material they required and price up the job themselves.

I do not have actual piecework prices or times of any shop work, so the following example from running shed times shows how the amount of bonus was allocated. At Old Oak Common in 1931, a firedropper was allowed thirty minutes for clearing the grate of each metro tank and other small shunting engines, and keeping the ashpits clear. He was allowed sixty minutes on the 4.6.0. classes, and on intermediate types forty-eight and fifty-four minutes, with the ROD 2.8.0. freight engines giving him ninety minutes – these times varied between the sheds, depending on the facilities available. In theory, if he worked hard he should accumulate time. For instance, if he had worked on six small locomotives at thirty minutes each and nine large ones at sixty minutes, his total achieved was twelve hours. So his day balance is 50 per cent because he had accumulated four hours beyond his eight actual hours worked, or a half again. If Jack Fleetwood's memory is correct, one eight-hour shift in the iron foundry involved a semi-skilled man preparing ten moulding boxes and packing (with sand), so as to cast five or six locomotive firebars per box. His piecework time allowance was ten hours, twenty-five minutes. Therefore, the time difference for him equals 30 per cent. A good weekly balance (the final entitlement), in the case of a factory man at least, would be around 50 per cent but an average was around 35 per cent of the flat rate, or about 16s for a skilled man in the 1930s. Jack said the average balance figure was more like 50 per cent by the middle of the war, and

The full Works Committee in session in the Mechanic Institute conference room in 1959. (Author's collection)

in the 1950s the unions had negotiated conditions whereby much higher payments again could be achieved.

The wages office clerks totalled up the figures and converted them to percentages payable to each man, then sent them on to the machine office. The fortnightly piecework account was calculated by Muldivo automatic electric calculators, from information on the piecework certificates. There were thirteen female operators who had to be kept fully occupied, so as to ensure the machines – at a cost of £150 each – were profitable. Unfortunately these electric calculators had to be imported from Italy and worked on the unfamiliar metric system. The female operatives, after intense training, became highly skilled and articulate with this system. For instance, they had to be able to decimalise pound sterling at sight to six decimal places. Of the three copies of each certificate received by the operatives, two were returned to the shop after checking and evaluation – one to the chargeman and one to the shop office for cross-referencing. During the four-weekly accounting period, a further large number of calculations were performed by the Muldivos, arising out of manufacturing costs, process accounts output, overhead charges, South Wales docks wages and statistics.

The detail piecework rates were constantly under review by both sides. The men might claim that a time allowance was, in practice, unprofitable and therefore as a gang they could not achieve their quota. Changing work practices or revised wage rates might also cause the men to seek a review of the piecework rates, but they knew that if they made too much fuss the work-study people would be brought in. Although the piecework committee was expected to settle differences, I have several letters showing that the chief mechanical engineer himself occasionally intervened. The CME's name usually appeared on noticeboard circulars and letters relating to departmental working conditions. This added weight to the instruction. But it was one of the CME's immediate understudies who normally dealt with these matters. Senior engineers in the CME Dept are not often remembered in their role as staff managers, but both Mr Collett and Mr Stanier had, in turn, spent time on pay and piecework problems, so had the outdoor assistant Mr Crump. They would have to meet with the men's representatives, especially when the delicate matter of cutting the rates and bonuses was necessary. According to letters between the depots and the management at Swindon,

There were three types of electric Muldivo calculators used at Swindon from 1936; earlier models were hand operated. Moldivo was the name of the British importer and distributor. (*GWR Magazine*)

piecework problems were expected to be sorted out locally and when Swindon did intervene, they did not usually settle things in favour of the men. Altering detail piecework prices was not something the company entered into lightly (see letter opposite from Mr Rodda, divisional superintendent at Worcester who became works manager at Wolverhampton Loco, Carriage & Wagon Works in 1929). Whilst pay rates were largely decided independently, the company presided over all other payments, unless they formed part of a nationally agreed wage settlement. In the early days when the Great Western had a choice, they dispensed the pay every two weeks, and of course they wished to minimise the man hours they had to devote to pay. Piecework payments, being an independent arrangement, could not be legislated upon, so they maintained the fortnightly payout.

Despite all the man hours spent compiling the figures, piecework was a clever way of the company achieving maximum output. No gang wanted a reputation for consistently achieving less than other gangs and therefore reducing the overall balance. Those receiving piecework payments saw them as a bit extra but it merely masked the fact that the basic wage was too low. The other reason to make up the wages with bonuses and allowances was that it made the men think twice before taking time off sick. A day rate was paid as an alternative to piece rate

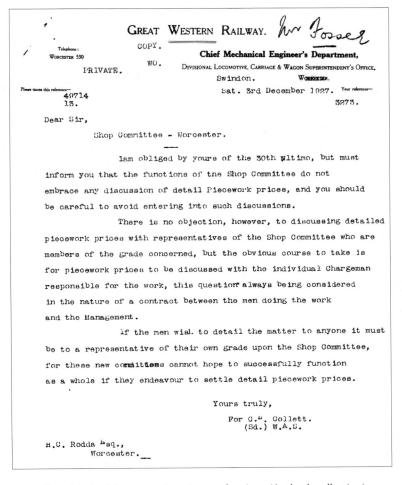

Letter from Mr Rodda concerning piecework prices. (Author's collection)

in certain cases where the nature of the work was such that the individual had no influence over his work rate. He received his bonus as a fixed 13.75 per cent of his flat wage. Day rate workers included watchmen, gatemen, cranemen, electricians, beltmen and WC attendants – the latter two had been phased out by the 1940s.

Besides the overtime and night rate of time-and-a-quarter, and Sunday and public holiday rate of time-and-a-half, certain work attracted other financial allowances for permanent and temporary staff, much of which had been agreed and subsequently modified at sectional council or workshop committee level. Conditions attached to wage increases often included the loss of an allowance, and so the dirty work allowance was discontinued in the 1920s. Individual cases where conditions were particularly unpleasant were still considered for extra payment by the local committees. A bonus of 3s was paid to men who formed part of a 'breakdown gang'. On each occasion, they were called upon to go out with the breakdown train in an emergency. Normal overtime payments were of course paid in addition to the call out payment if the crew was required outside of the normal working day. Where men who were not regular members of a breakdown gang were called upon to augment those rerailing an engine or vehicle, or clearing debris from the track, they were also entitled to the 3s bonus. Outstation men often worked longer days or nights and could claim travelling and breakdown time where applicable, as well as the food and lodging allowance, which was 2s 6d per week before the war.

The shopmen could not claim the allowances for food and lodging like some conciliation grades who worked away from home, and no doubt this was pointed out by the men when negotiating on piecework. Before nationalisation, there was a small annual payment made to the qualified first aider of the shop. With this, he had to replace all the supplies he used, such as bandages, iodine, absorbent lint and smelling salts. The remainder might cover some of the piecework bonus he would lose while doing ambulance training and practising first aid. He also received an extra free travel pass every time he passed the annual test. Technical, clerical and supervisory staff could claim travelling expenses when on company business and lodging expenses when away from their home districts on relief duties. Items claimed in personal expense accounts and entered in the paybill as petty disbursements might be travelling, laundry, postal and telephone charges, removal allowance and cab hire for conveyance of cash to and from the bank. Allowances and enhanced rates for clerical staff and most other grades in the CME Dept were given for temporary duty in a higher grade, lodging and travelling. Only cost-of-living allowances, and not reimbursements, were classed as earnings, therefore they were included with sick and holiday pay.

Another way a bit extra could be made was for a worker to come up with a way of increasing efficiency in his workplace. A 'Suggestion Scheme' had been in operation on the GWR since 1913, the first on any British railway. A financial benefit was offered if a person could convince his superiors his idea would save the company money. There was always scope for improving working methods to reduce paperwork, speed up production or reduce the amount of scrap (known at Swindon as 'shxxxers'). Carefully drawn diagrams with text were required for consideration by a committee, and to avoid any prejudice the identity of the person submitting a suggestion was not disclosed. The scheme was apparently a long drawn-out process. In some cases men put forward ideas directly to their foreman, who then took all the credit for it. This caused resentment and consequently suppressed further efforts.

The system of adjusting wages that was used in the 1930s had started during the war when inflation was high and the railways were under state control. Before that, the GWR had prepared their own graph showing the rise and fall of the cost of living as determined by Board of Trade statistics, which they used to adjust the wages. Wages were higher in the 1920s than in the '30s because of inflation caused by the First World War, but of course the buying power of currency was reduced. During this period, the Ministry of Labour was publishing a cost-of-living index (COLI) number based on a quarterly review. The GWR, like other British railways, was bound by the index and would adjust the cost-of-living allowance (usually referred to as the 'war wage bonus') accordingly. This was known as the 'sliding scale arrangement'. The lowest paid grades were given special consideration, more so than they were over the cuts in the standard wage rates between 1928 and 1936. The datum figure, or index number at which the bonus became payable, was set lower for those on the lower rates. Wages had been falling steadily with the sliding scale arrangement since a peak in late 1920, and the COLI reached its lowest level (compared to the base line year of 1914) during the recession of early 1930s. Up until July 1938 the index had not been above sixty since the first few weeks of the decade.

Management and government hoped the sliding scale arrangement would break the cycle of what they saw as unreasonable demands followed by disruption. As early as 1924 it seemed that this might not be the case and moved an anonymous correspondent to write a piece in the *GWR Magazine* in response to unrest. The writer pointed out the financial advantage was already offered to railwaymen and that railway pay rates compared very well to the other great industries, so much that there was a tendency for the position of railwaymen to be held up as an argument for improving conditions in other trades. He also pointed out that the shopmen lost a smaller percentage of their war wage when the COLI went down (shopmen's wage adjustments were not linked to the sliding scale). He implied that the rank and file should remain loyal to the company during a downturn in its fortunes, and warned of the very real danger that increased wages expenditure could mean job cuts and increases in fares. The popular monthly *GWR Magazine* was produced at Paddington and the editor was appointed from the general manager's staff. Felix Pole said in *His Book* that 'The G.W.R. magazine played an important part', referring to the family spirit being promoted by the company in the early 1920s. The publication of the professional and recreational achievements amongst all ranks, for a small subscription, undoubtedly improved the sense of family. When disputes became news, however, the widely read magazine's 'appeals to reason' must have eroded the men's support considerably.

In 1931 the Great Western, along with the other three British railway companies, the Southern, the London, Midland & Scottish and the London & North Eastern, applied to the wages board for a further reduction in wage rates, as the cost-of-living allowance had all but disappeared. Traffic and docks receipts continued to fall and reductions in the wages bill would help the railways to remain competitive – the first reduction in the gross wage had been agreed with the unions in August 1928 as a temporary measure! The rail unions and the national shopmen's council agreed to the cuts in return for some assurances against job cuts and reduced working. They also submitted other proposals to the board and to the railway companies for consideration, which were rejected. Officers and staff with salaries of £350 or more per annum had their normal pay increases deferred with the possibility of a reduction at a later date whilst Directors' fees, salaries and wages had already been reduced by 2.5 per cent during 1929–30. The conclusions of the National Wages Board, published in March 1931, included increased rates for conciliation and workshop grades in respect of day and night overtime, night duty, Sunday and public holidays, although with working hours being cut few would benefit in the foreseeable future. Only in cases where double time was previously paid was there a reduction in the rate to time-and-two-thirds. Conciliation grades had already lost 2.5 per cent on their basic earnings three years earlier. Now they would lose a further 2.5 per cent from earnings in excess of 40s per week. For example, a man earning 50s would lose a total of 1s 6d, made up as follows: 1s 3d being 2.5 per cent from the whole 50s, plus 3d being 2.5 per cent on the amount over 40s. Salaried staff wages had been reduced by the same amount. They would lose a further 2.5 per cent on earnings above £100 per year and workshop grades went from 2.5 per cent to a straight 4.25 per cent.

In 1932 a further reduction in its wages bill was the only solution to improving the company's financial position during this time of severe economic depression and to honour its commitment to shareholders. Railwaymen's salaries and wages in real terms were up 114 per cent compared to the base line year of 1914, the average increase outside the industry was only 70 per cent. The joint railway companies proposed an all round percentage reduction taking the amount to 10 per cent, and not surprisingly direct talks with the unions to this effect failed. The 10 per cent cut was never introduced because the wages boards never agreed to them, and there were no further moves to increase the reductions which, with 'partial restorations' lasted well into 1937. By 1938 the COLI had climbed back to 60 per cent above that of 1914, with 25,000 Western men receiving wage increases due to the reversal of the rate cuts and the sliding scale arrangement.

With every adjustment to the pay rates and bonuses, the CME Dept at Swindon Works' 'GW6' received notification from the general manager's office. Their accounts department then prepared new figures and a further letter was sent via the divisional running superintendents for the information of the local paybill staff. These letters explained how the changes would effect the various sections of workers in the department and were usually signed by the chief clerk, 'for the CME', otherwise signed by the outdoor assistant and sometimes principal assistant to the CME. Notices from the general manager for display at depots and cabins then followed.

Manual workers, and others whose remuneration did not exceed £250 per annum and who were not members of the GWR superannuation, or another similar scheme, had to subscribe to National Health and Pensions Insurance. Every insurable employee had to hand in to the company a current insurance card and pay a contribution each week. In 1936 men aged sixteen to sixty-five paid 10*d* and women paid 7*d* per week. The GWR matched the contribution making the individuals total stamp 1*s* 8*d* and 1*s* 2*d* respectively. If the insured employee was a member of either the GWR Staff Friendly Society or Locomotive Running Department Staff Approved Society, they would contribute 1*d* less and the employer 1*d* more. Sickness benefit (claimable after twenty-six weeks of contributions) was 9*s* per week for men, increasing to 15*s* after 104 weeks. Women's benefit was proportionately less. Thus all workers in the CME Dept became members of the Medical Fund Society (MFS) but Swindon people paid extra for facilities such as the dispensary and baths. Family men paid the maximum 10*d* per week and this also covered any children under sixteen, whilst retired members without dependants paid the least, a halfpenny, allowing them all access to a whole range of medical and health services, unlike any other schemes anywhere else in the country. The book *A Century of Medical Service*, a history of the MFS, shows the subscription figures for 1947 had remained unchanged from the 1930s. This may be because in the later period, prior to the takeover by the National Health Service, the fee was separate from sick pay deduction. Bernard Darwin's extensive account also gives the company's contribution to the MFS as £1,750 for the year 1947. On top of this, the company alone, and not the subscriptions, paid the salaries of the medical staff. Later came the National (Health) Insurance, which George remembers paying as a fixed amount of 6*s* 9*d* in the mid-1950s.

Those same employees whose total rate of remuneration was £250 per annum or less (in 1936) had to be insured against unemployment – with very few exceptions, all outside the CME Dept. When the worker commenced employment, he or she had to obtain an unemployment book from the Labour Exchange and hand it to the company. Again the rate for unemployment insurance was 10*d*, to which the employer also contributed 10*d*, with women and juniors paying slightly less. National Health, Pensions and Unemployment (known collectively as National Insurance) contributions were payable every week that wages were received, including paid holidays and sick leave with pay. The other compulsory deduction was income tax, of which the paybill clerks were frequently reminded of the importance of entering, each week, the necessary particulars on wages income tax cards. Occasionally the company was advised of a court order, taken out against a man to retrieve unpaid loans or fines through the paybill.

The apparent free privileges offered to Great Western men – the reduced rail fares, the apprenticing of a worker's son or the cheap coal and wood – came at a price, regardless of whether the man and his family took them up or not. Up until 1927 the men in the workshops had been paid according to rates set by their various crafts throughout the industry. Because these rates were calculated outside the company where privileges were not given, a fixed sum deduction was made as a 'differential'.

A person might owe for coal and firewood or scrap timber provided by the company for private use, and this was deducted automatically every balance week. The various deductions were calculated to be taken either weekly, such as health insurance, unemployment insurance and savings bank, or fortnightly, such as coal, wood, life insurance, medical fund and Railway Benevolent Institution. Gas supplied by the company for household use and the mechanics subscription was deducted every four weeks. Railway convalescent home subs were deducted every three months and the Casualty Fund, annually.

Membership of the Mechanics Institute was readily subscribed to by most Swindon workers. Between the wars, 4*d* a week allowed them and their families to apply for a free pass and travel on one of the annual 'Trip Holiday' trains. The Works Committee objected to membership to participate in 'Trip' and after the war this was no longer required. Unlimited reduced rail fares, known as 'privileged tickets', were available to all employees and covered the workman's trains. After the war railway staff commuted to 'the factory' free of charge. Besides 'Trip', one further free travel pass was given to each employee at that time. This was increased after nationalisation and included one or two British Railways (known as 'foreigners') passes in 1949, depending on the length of service. A card was issued to past and present employees, authorising them to obtain free and privileged tickets at the Works' booking office from 10.30

to 11.00 any weekday morning. The Helping Hand Fund had been aiding deserving cases amongst the past and present workers since 1924. They held fund-raising events and collected contributions, then allocated financial assistance where needed. It was claimed to be the only scheme of its kind on any British railway. As with other optional charity contributions, the worker could opt to have payments deducted at source. If he chose not to give, this remained confidential. The famous male voice choir, GWR (Accounts) Staff Gleemen, were sufficiently popular to record some of their songs for the Parlophone Company in the early 1930s. They donated the royalties from sales to the GWR Helping Hand Fund.

I have attempted to cover only a selection of organisations offering benefits to Swindon railwaymen. The GWR Loco and Carriage Department Sick Fund Society at 6 & 7 Oxford Street was the approved society for health and pension insurance, and about 50 per cent of local railway staff belonged to it. For a fee of around 6*d* a week the wise investor could insure he got by, if and when he found himself 'out on the club'. There was no shortage of private insurance available for accident, unemployment, retirement and death. The 'Boilermakers Iron and Steel Shipbuilders Society' had a local branch secretary in Swindon to deal with industrial injury compensation, as did other staff and trade associations, and successful claims were paid via the railway's wages department. The GWR itself organised various pension and benevolent funds. There was an arrangement between 'The Ocean Accident and Guarantee Corporation' and *GWR Magazine* whereby the subscriber paid an extra 1*d* for the insurance edition of the monthly magazine, and received a range of death and accident coverage while working or travelling on the GWR.

Subject to a medical examination, all salaried staff were required to join a pension scheme, such as the Great Western Railway Salaried Staff Supplemental Pension Fund, the GWR Salaried Staff Retiring Allowances Fund or the GWR Female Clerks Pension Fund. The employee paid between 4 to 6.75 per cent of their salary from the time of joining a scheme until their retirement, with the company contributing a like amount. The fixed percentage contribution depended on how old they were when they joined, and no one was admitted as a new member over the age of thirty-nine years. Every member who attained the age of sixty was, on leaving the service, entitled to a capital sum and an annuity for life. The amount of the superannuation allowances depended of course upon the completed years of membership.

In July 1941 the various pension and superannuation funds, including the GWR Engineman and Fireman's Mutual Assurance Sick and Superannuation Society, became known collectively as The GWR Superannuation Fund. The next of kin of a superannuated man who was 'called up' received the difference between his forces pay and his normal railway pay, less the superannuation contribution. When it became clear the war was not going to finish quickly, the directors of the company, as trustees, suspended all new applications from about 1942. George Petfield, along with all new appointments at that time, had to wait until 1945 to join the Fund. George remembers some of his colleagues joining the London & North Eastern Railway (LNER) scheme after nationalisation because of improved terms. Many men with families paid into the Widows and Orphans Fund to ensure some financial cover in the event of their own death. The shopmen did not have a superannuation scheme until as late as 1954.

4

PAYBILL PRODUCTION

From September 1936, the start of the morning shift in the workshops was changed to 7.55 a.m. instead of 8.00 a.m., Monday to Saturday. The factory hooter was sounded an hour before the start time in the morning, presumably to wake people up. Then there were two short blasts, ten minutes and five minutes before the start of the morning and afternoon shifts, and a longer blast at the start time. Dinnertime was one hour, which started from 12.30 p.m.. The afternoon shift finished at 5.30 p.m., except Saturday when the working day finished at 12 noon. The system at Swindon allowed the man in the workshops up to half an hour after the last hooter to 'book on', with loss of pay of course, but after that he was sent home for the day. All latecomers had to see the foreman before starting work, knowing that he had the authority to dismiss him at any moment over bad timekeeping. Most of the men were rarely, if ever, late or off with sickness, and many shops had someone that claimed never to have had a day out ill in all their years 'inside'. Peter Reade's old foreman Mr Titcomb retired from the stamping shop in 1949. He had completed fifty-one years of service, without a single week's absence through illness.

The method of recording the men's attendance and punctuality in the Swindon workshops was by allocating each a brass time check, sometimes referred to as a 'tally' or 'ticket', stamped with his paybill number. The idea presumably originated in the mining industries, where metal checks and boards were used extensively for recording the workers' attendances. A board with numbered hooks to hang the checks was fixed to the wall near the entrance to the shop – larger shops had more than one board. The checkboards varied in size and design but they could all be closed with a glass cover. Most were counter-balanced and pulled up and down like a sash window. Like all the wooden fittings and fixtures 'inside', they would have been made by the Work's carpenters.

Before the final hooter sounded for the start of the shift, each person would be required to remove his check (and only his check) and retain it. The 'checky' (spelling varies), usually a shop labourer, was responsible for closing the glass cover at the start of the shift, thereby excluding all latecomers. Coloured penalty checks, showing a quarter or half an hour's pay to be forfeited, would be placed on the hook of anyone not conforming to this procedure, unless they were on nights, working away or their timekeeping was being recorded by the time office, in which case, alternative checks would cover their hooks in their absence. In Edwardian times 'losing a quarter' or 'a half' meant not being allowed to start until after the breakfast or dinner break. At the end of the shift, the men would have to return the checks, which in reality were thrown at the wooden tray beneath the board – many missed the tray as they hurried passed. The poorly paid checky, who gladly worked extra on either end of the shift to earn a little more, would retrieve all the checks and return them to the correct hooks. The checkboard system was, according to the company rule book, 'worked according

A workshop checkboard. Written on the back of this photo is 'T' shop 9/2/09. There are two sets of numbers painted on the board, so perhaps the adjoining machine shop used it too. *(Author's collection)*

to local arrangements'. The only condition from Paddington was that the checks never left the premises. This had not always been the case. Years earlier, the checks were handed in when the owner was at work and kept by him after knocking off.

After the commencement of the shift, the time office personnel would record the remaining checks and note any penalty or alternative checks placed on the hooks by the checky. This information was then compiled at one of the time offices. The loco side offices were East, West, and Rodbourne Lane – there was another on the 'carriage side', as well as one for the running shed. George Petfield doesn't remember receiving the timekeeping records from the time offices, only direct from the chargemen of the shop, so he assumes the system was altered before 1951. Completed paybill sheets were returned to the shop offices every week to be signed by the foreman, who did not always have the inclination to check too closely what he was signing. The chargeman also used the checkboard to determine the attendance when compiling the piecework sheets; Jack Fleetwood's chargehand in the iron foundry would withhold some of the piecework account 'in the back of the book', then claim extra for the men before Christmas and 'Trip'. Up until the late 1940s, the timecheck was also required to be handed to the lavatory attendant when going to the toilet, as a maximum of ten minutes was allowed – over that and a quarter of an hour's pay was lost.

Salaried staff did not have to use a checkboard system, and their start and finish times were staggered slightly from the shops. All salaried staff in the workshops were required to sign in at one of the time offices before the start of the shift in the morning. Some workers on irregular shifts, such as maintenance engineers and those not allocated to a particular shop, were required to use the check system in use at one of the time offices. There was an unwritten law that allowed staff grades to arrive up to two minutes late and leave two minutes early, whilst the men in the shops expected to wash their hands and perhaps change their outer clothes during work time before going home. The use of the checkboards for timekeeping at Swindon Works lasted right up until about 1970 when time stamp clocks were brought in. These were nothing new and had been in limited use elsewhere on the Western for many years. The Works had tried clock and punchcard machines well before the 1930s, but the idea was not taken up, probably because the early design was unreliable. The fire station did use a time clock recorder, one of the few places in the Works to do so. As an office boy in the east time office in 1953, Alan Lambourn would go and collect the clock rolls from there once a week.

An amusing story recalled in the *Swindon Railway News* involved Mr K.J. Cook, who was at the time the loco works manager. The story goes that 'K.J.C.' came into the shop and noticed an area of floor near the checkboard had sunk a little and remarked with a smile that it was 'probably due to all you chaps hanging about round the checkboard at the end of the day waiting for the hooter to blow'. He didn't get away with that one. 'Tent caused by the weight o' money we gets, any'ow,' said a voice from the rear.

At outstation sites, where the men were not required to sign on and off duty, the inspector, foreman or chargeman was held responsible for collecting the forms (timesheets). In some situations the men themselves signed the forms and the person in charge noted any lateness, overtime and leave; sometimes they phoned in the details to their workshop. A signed copy of hours worked was returned to the individual before payday and he had to have it ready for inspection if required when collecting his pay. Whenever possible, arrangements were made for the outstation gangs to sign on and off under the supervision of a local station or department, if they were not arriving direct from Swindon.

At the Works on the day before payday, checky would collect paychecks from the cash office. The person issuing these checks was provided with a 'tick list' of the men's names and numbers corresponding with the paybill so any necessary corrections could be made. The checky, or other designated person, was responsible for distributing the checks and satisfying himself as to the identity of the payees. By the 1930s paychecks in use were mainly made of copper. The stores' checks were invariably of alloy and referred to as 'whitemetal checks'. Some shops had the checks drilled so that they could be collected from the checkboard on payday. As with the timechecks, each had the pay number stamped on the face. Blocks of numbers were allocated permanently to each shop and not to the workman. The 100 or so workers in the iron foundry had pay numbers from 5,700, the chair foundry from 6,000 and the brass foundry from 6,100 and so on – not all sets of numbers were as many as four digits. Jack Fleetwood remembers that, in the early days, a charge of 5s was made if a man lost his check. In later years, 'ole checky' always seemed to have a few blanks that could be dye stamped, thus avoiding the charge. Clerical, supervisory and other salaried staff did not have to hand in a paycheck, but they still needed a registered pay number. All paybills were identified by a recipient's name and number which would be required from the payee in any discussion with the wages department.

In 1951, George, by now a Grade 4, moved to the loco wages office. This occupied the top floor of the old loco managers block. The carriage side of the wages office was also in close proximity to their managers offices in the Carriage & Wagon (C&W) Works. The only time the two sets of staff worked together, prior to the amalgamation in June 1952, was during the paying out when all available staff were used to cover every shop simultaneously. The loco wages office was split into various sections: George was in Bert Broad's section, one of three dealing with the loco works. Other sections covered mechanical productions, motive power, salaried staff and stores. Each had eight people, including a section chief, and two large desks were positioned side by side with four people working each side. Staff worked in pairs. George worked with Kathleen Foster who had recently moved over from the C&W wages office. They later became husband and wife. Between them they would deal with all the timesheets sent in from the iron, brass and (track) chair foundries and they were also responsible for issuing pay numbers to the new starters in those areas. The office as a whole was responsible for about 5,500 shop-based workers alone, so it was quite a coincidence that George dealt with Jack Fleetwood's timesheet in his earliest days in the loco wages office. Whether George was born with it or developed a great capacity for detail due to his work, I do not know, but if I asked him if he remembered someone in a workshop fifty years ago, not only was he likely to say 'yes', but he would often give their pay number as well. For instance, the three men in the oxygen plant then were Alfie Church, Alf Dunman and chargeman Arthur Stanley, numbers 3476, 3479 and 3410 respectively.

The loco and carriage wages offices both moved into the CME block when they amalgamated. The carriage wages was now in the old 'make up' area next to the cash office with Senior Clerk Billy Gunter and the loco office was across the corridor on the east side of the building. There was now one clerk in overall charge of the two, collectively known as the central wages office. This was Bill Sargeant with Fred Hook and, shortly afterwards, Luke Roberts as his assistant. Mr Roberts was still looking after the administration of the wartime Comforts Fund, which was being continued to assist the casualties who were still in the hospital or at home. George's first section in central wages (loco) included George Tomes, who was in charge, Ray Jackson and Oliver Porter. He still dealt with wages staff timesheets, and now K.C. (coppersmiths) and K.T. (tinsmiths) shops, also stamping and steam hammers, a total of about 250 workers.

The clerks worked 6ft apart at double desks. Their only aids were 'Ready Reckoners' (books of rate tables) and adding machines, of which each office had two or possibly three. Timesheets and piecework sheets were sent in from the workshops, and clerks working in pairs would work out the individual entitlements and stoppages and add the totals in spaces provided on the sheets. They would first calculate the gross pay according to the individual's rate, then from that the percentage tax deductible using tax tables and the individual's tax code. Then together with the piecework bonus, overtime and more than thirty types of possible deductions, the totals were transferred onto 'wages cost-slips'. The slips were then sent on to the machine room as 'time returns', the same system used for material costs. The methods used to arrive at these figures had not changed for many years, except as George Petfield said:

> By the time I started in the wages office, the information from the timesheets went straight onto Powers punchcards. The punchcards were as they had always been, approximately 7in x 3in with the workers ticket number printed on them. They worked on the Hollerith system whereby pencil marks would indicate where the combination of holes were to be made by the machine, very similar to the modern lottery tickets. A second card used throughout the year kept a running total for each person.

In the wages office you got to get out and about a bit more than in other types of accounts work. If there was a problem with a timesheet, George usually found it easier to go and see the worker who had submitted it. However, this was not always possible because many discrepancies were due to excess payments claimed by outstation workers. These men did not have their timesheets checked like the shopmen, where any such problems should have been picked up by the shop clerk. They relied on the foreman to check when he signed it, but he was less thorough than the clerk. If the workman was not happy with his pay, he might go along to the office, where the relevant clerk could usually point out why he had not received what was anticipated. Sometimes a little extra overtime payment took the man into the next tax bracket, making him liable for a higher rate of tax on the whole amount. Understandably, he then felt cheated and thought twice before volunteering for extra work next time. The rate of tax increased at 5s intervals in the 1940s and '50s.

At paybill offices all across the system, the figures for the CME workers were compiled based on their own recognised method of timekeeping. The time returns were sent on to the divisional or chief officer, together with the correct coded form detailing any absences due to annual leave, special leave and sickness. Anticipated hours worked could be added to the time returns (now usually referred to as the paybills), as the paybills for the period after 6 p.m. on a Friday were forwarded before the end of the working week. If a worker estimated hours turned out to be different than the actual hours, the divisional or district officer had to be advised by first thing Monday morning via the coded form, so that if possible the paybill could be amended before being sent to the chief accountant at Swindon. If it was not possible to amend the paybill, any over-entry had to be deducted at the pay table and the amount paid back through the daily cash account.

'No.40' office in the 1930s. The machinery section was behind the photographer. The two girls in the front are Nancy Verrinder (left) and Molly Adkins. Behind them are Marjorie Gooding (left) and Ethel Fletcher. Next row back are Beryldene Hunt (left) and Enid Munden. (Fred Stevens's collection)

Producing the weekly paybill was a problem of recurring urgency at the Works. This is how the Western Region described the biggest commitment at Swindon outside of manufacturing, George said:

> Everyone involved with wages knew their duty. It was the one job in the factory that must not and did not get behind. Consequently, overtime in the Wages Sections was not something regularly required to allow catching up. If anyone involved with wages was off sick or on holiday, their work had to be covered and the deadlines met. The rate of sickness was very low in our department and sometimes staff struggled in when they were clearly not fit. There was psychological pressure to do your share and not to leave it to your colleagues – besides the 'Sick Record' was always a factor in assessment for promotion.

Despite the importance of the work, George felt there was a tendancy for others to look down on wages work, 'that was until they came to work here', he said.

Liz Bartlett (*née* Ribbins) worked in this office for a while and remembers her section included Malcolm Avenell, George Petfield and Walt Shepperd. Other clerks in the office in the early 1950s included Frank Horn, Clem White, Ashley Manhair, Reg Drake, Mike Cousins, Eric (Tub) Loveday (who could take off radio comic Tony Hancock), Eric Martin, Dave Bunce, Percy Harris, and Bob Fox from Weymouth. Amongst them there was a beekeeper, a Shakespearian actor and a flying instructor. Several were members of the Railway Correspondence and Travel Society and one was a football referee (elsewhere in accounts another amateur referee had handled an FA Cup Final and an Amateur Cup final in the 1920s). Dave Bunce ran an office shop, supplying biscuits and chocolate at cost price. George said that this sort of thing had to be conducted very discreetly and would not have been tolerated by management at all. Mike Cousins bussed in fourteen miles every day from Lechlade. The small Gloucestershire town had a station, and in fact his father was the station master there, but there was no direct rail route.

George remembers some of his colleagues for the military campaigns they fought or the regiments they were attached to. This impressed the younger generation in those days. One fellow was at the Dardanelles, another at Gallipoli; others were remembered as Ex-Royal Engineers or Royal Artillery. Some bore physical or mental scars, but most continued working until normal retirement age. Fred Boucher had been a Navy regular before arriving in the loco wages office during the Second World War. Fred had been injured during the Battle of the River Plate and despite continuing ill health, spent thirty years in the department. One poor fellow suffered from a speech impediment due to shell shock in the First World War, but was still in the Works' offices forty years later. Another casualty from the 'first lot', Frank Witts, arrived back at the office very late after dinner one day. He said he had jumped off the bus at the medical centre and his lower leg prosthesis came off, causing a female nearby to faint and leaving him to deal with both problems at the same time. Walter Sheppard and Reg Drake were typical of many clerks who had been in the accounts department. since before 1914; they had done their bit in the Royal Flying Corps. Many young men in the Works were recruited into aircraft production in the First World War; others arrived at Swindon for the first time following the rundown of the Air Force at the war's end.

Swearing was rarely heard, unless something went very wrong, and was usually directed at someone on the other end of the phone, then followed an apology all round, especially pronounced if females were nearby. For some reason in those days there were few women, or 'W2's as they were known to the company, in loco wages compared to other areas.

When the boss was out of the office, some people would make private calls. George remembers one chap entertaining the office as he became ever more irate with someone in the booking office at the station. The 'imbecile' kept quoting him times of trains to Lemster and he wanted to go to *Leominster*. On another occasion, the calm of the office was shattered when someone rang the AE shop office looking for Mr Duck, the clerk in charge. 'I understand you've got a duck down there called Mr Clerk,' began the enquirer quite innocently. There was always a mix of characters who broke the monotony: the quiet one with the very dry sense of humour; the practical joker; the extravert and the shy and nervous types. One chap had a habit of kicking his shoes off under the desk when working. Knowing him as a rather sober, aloof type who would be unimpressed by the joke, someone managed to get the shoes away and hide them. 'Next thing, the victim was summoned by the Works' accountant to undertake a special job,' said George, but still no one owned up to the prank. He eventually turned up for the appointment in a tatty old pair of shoes he kept in his locker. On his return, of course, the other pair of shoes were back under his desk. George's time in this office ended with computerisation, which made much of the work done by the wages offices obsolete.

Mechanised accounting was divided into CME accounts, stores or mileage office machine rooms. All accounts came under the control of the chief, then later the regional accountant at Paddington. Nearly 40,000 paybills and payslips were totalled up and printed by machines in the CME Accounts for the carriage and wagon engineers, chief accountants, chief mechanical and electrical engineers and motive power superintendent's departments. Each had sections dealing with paybills, as well as with pensions, retirements, free and privileges tickets. The stores superintendent's department was also based in the CME offices but had separate accounts sections.

Percy Richards MBE, a senior clerk at Swindon in the 1930s and '40s, presented a paper to the GWR Engineering Society entitled 'The Application of Modern Machines to the Production of Accounts and Costs of the Chief Mechanical Engineers Department'. He said:

In the early 1900s, the Accounts were kept in bound books, written with elaborate copperplate figures. Next came the 'Slip System' which, by means of separate documents for wages and materials expended on each job, made it possible to analyse expenditure by hand sorting of the slips. Later again, the Company was persuaded that the 'punched card system' was so far advanced as to make an extended trial desirable, if it was to keep abreast of the times. Up until then, the question of capital outlay was measured only in terms of clerks and stationery. The first experiments with machines were applied to the costing of repairs

The loco wages office some time between 1952–1956. Fred Boucher and Walter Sheppard are in the centre, facing the photographer. The section dealing with workshop stores was off to the left. (BR National Railway Museum)

to individual engines, boilers and tenders. These were done by Powers-Samas machines and proved eminently satisfactory.

Indeed, Barbara Carter still associates the Powers-Samas accounting machines with the different stages of loco repair costs from her time there in the 1940s, and they were also used for material costs. Other mechanised accounting covered train schedules, fuel costs, goods inwards, stores transactions, statistics, manufacturing costs and so on. A Hollerith punchcard sorter and tabulator had been in use at Swindon since before the First World War. Barbara said that 'an early tabulator with a mechanical starting handle was kept at the back of our office, I remember working on it in the 1940s'.

Swindon was one of the very few industrial sites prepared to invest in the best equipment and training to achieve efficient accounting. Indeed, the company is thought to have been the first railway in this country to have used the advanced Powers-Samas system. They were, however, reluctant at first to be influenced by the early successes of outside firms and apply the technology to paybills because, having so many variable deductions, paybill figures had always been difficult to mass produce. The numerous deductions due to so many additional facilities offered to employees and the varying periods between collection made the GWR system particularly complicated. Mr Richards said, 'Now [1936] with something approaching £30,000 invested in these machines in the last seven years, it will be appreciated how much of a reasonable return on the outlay can be shown'. It is not possible to ascertain from this account, or probably any other source, the chronological development of punchcard application to paybills. Although Mr Richards does say that 'the production of the weekly paybills at Swindon had still not quite reached the full potential of the Powers-Samas punched-card capability, but was going through the final stages of trial'.

Cost slips arrived from the wages offices where they had been priced and evaluated, and costs made to balance with the paybill totals. Now referred to as paybills, they were the

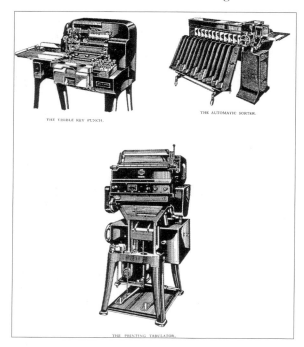

THE VISIBLE KEY PUNCH.

THE AUTOMATIC SORTER.

THE PRINTING TABULATOR.

Powers-Samas punchcard machines used at Swindon in the 1930s and '40s for paybills and material charges. Service mechanics and electricians employed by Powers-Samas were permanently on site. (*GWR Magazine*)

The machine room paybill section, Christmas 1953 or '54. Left to right, standing: Barbara Tuck, Mary Beckhelling-Williams, Bill Sargeant, Audrey Sharland, Fred Hook (from loco wages office), Liz Bartlett (*née* Ribbins), Janet Hooper, Doreen Freeman. Left to right, sitting: Betty Fincham, Florence Gapper, Rosie Jones and Doreen Huff. (Liz Bartlett)

The gang assigned to the preparation of the Royal Engine 4082 *Windsor Castle* prior to the funeral of King George V. The royal coat of arms would be fitted to the locomotive running plate, one on either side. 'A' shop in January 1936. (Author's collection)

Liz Bartlett was the clerk chosen to be photographed with the new computer in 1957. She is about to place cards punched with basic data into the magazine. They were processed at the rate of two per second and arrived in the receiver at the front end. (Liz Bartlett)

figures for the period up until the previous Saturday lunchtime. The information was then transferred to punchcards using semi-automatic punching machines. The cards then contained a combination of holes representing a person's gross pay. Any mistakes made to the punchcards by the machines could be corrected using a hand punch. Other punched cards were set up for fixed and variable deductions. These were added and tabulator machines converted the information on the cards back to numbers and figures.

By 1936 the actual production of the paybill giving a net figure for payment and a cash slip was performed by three Underwood-Sundstrand accounting and payroll machines. The earlier model of the Underwood-Sundstrand calculator required the completed paybills to go through a Burroughs listing machine for production of the payslip. Each shop in turn was handed over to an operator who took information from a combination of timesheets, machine cards and deductions list. The printed bills were returned to the wages offices to be checked and finally sent on, two days before payday, to the chief accountant and chief cashier. A summary sheet accompanied each batch of bills and detailed the total cash to be drawn. Paybills were also produced for money due for pensions and retirement allowances.

The latest electric calculating machines were installed at Swindon Works from the early 1930s, starting with Comptometers and, for the piecework figures, the Muldivo calculators. Previously, the ladies had been using mechanical Comptometer adding and calculator machines which were retained and used in the mileage office for many more years. The machine room also contained National Ellis listing machines, Ormig duplicators, Electromatic typewriters and addressograph machines, which printed names and pay numbers onto blank (skeleton) paybills and timesheets.

The electronic machine room in 1957. As well as the PCC in the background, there was a key punch, a sorter, interpolator, a reproducer, an interpreter and two tabulators. (BR National Railway Museum)

Liz Bartlett started work in the paybill machine room in the early 1950s at the age of seventeen. It was, by then, separate from the other CME mechanised accounts behind the cash office on the east side of the ground floor. She used National Cash Register machines, but not all work here was automated. Liz said:

> Amongst other things, girls at desks had to work out the 'cash analysis' for the cash office, others had to stick stamps on National Insurance Cards. Shortly after I arrived we amalgamated with the Carriage and Wagon side. Mr (Bill) Sargent was in charge of the new central wages machine rooms and Miss Gapper was my Section Chief.

The Western Region was among the first undertakings in the British Commonwealth to make a complete study of electronic accounting. Powers-Samas of Croyden manufactured and, as a combined effort with engineers from Swindon, installed electronic accounting machines in the railway works. A new machine room was set up next to the carriage wages office in the old 'cash make up' area. The British-made Electronic Multiplying Punch (EMP) was the first electronic machine obtained. It began running in 1954, 'requiring only a few minutes training'. The installation of the Powers-Samas 'programme controlled computer' was behind schedule. 'So as an interim measure, a Hollerith computer was installed, which was quite straightforward,' said Liz Bartlett. George, in the wages office, was not so keen on the temporary equipment:

> We had to stay late one night awaiting some figures from 'the Hollerith'. We waited till 9.15 p.m. then went over to 'The Locomotive' Public House, and had a pint. When we returned there was

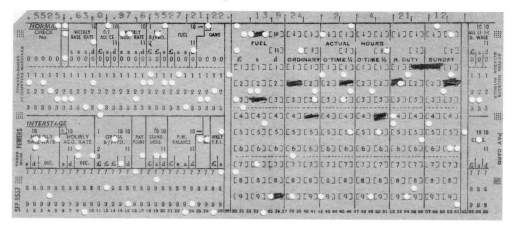

The later Powers–Samas punchcard, the medium by which large volumes of information was processed. The style and size of the cards changed little from the 1930s until they became obsolete after 1959. (Author's collection)

The first electronic accounting machine, the EMP, served to emphasise the advantages that could be gained through the introduction of a computer. (BR National Railway Museum)

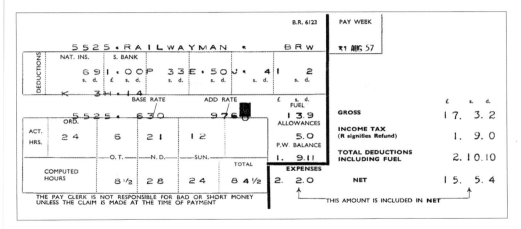

							B.R. 6123	PAY WEEK		

DEDUCTIONS

5 5 2 5 . R A I L W A Y M A N   •   B R W   ₹1 AUG 57

NAT. INS.	S. BANK				
6 9	1 . O O	P 3 3	E . 5 O	J . 4	2
s. d.	£ s. d.	s. d.	s. d.	s. d.	s. d.

K   3 H . 1 4

	BASE RATE		ADD RATE		£ s. d. FUEL

ORD.   5 5 2 5 .   6 3 0   9 7 6 0 █   1 3.9

					ALLOWANCES
ACT. HRS.	2 4	6	2 1	1 2	5.O

P.W. BALANCE   1.   9.11

	O.T.	N.D.	SUN.	TOTAL	EXPENSES
COMPUTED HOURS	8 ½	2 8	2 4	8 4 ½	2. 2.O

GROSS   £   s.   d.
                    1 7.   3. 2

INCOME TAX
(R signifies Refund)   1.   9. 0

TOTAL DEDUCTIONS
INCLUDING FUEL   2. 1 0.1O

NET   1 5.   5. 4

THE PAY CLERK IS NOT RESPONSIBLE FOR BAD OR SHORT MONEY UNLESS THE CLAIM IS MADE AT THE TIME OF PAYMENT

THIS AMOUNT IS INCLUDED IN **NET**

A sample payslip for 1957. (Author's collection)

still nothing forthcoming so I went home at midnight. Ron Alexander and another clerk stayed till 4.00 a.m. so they could get the information needed and not hold up the paybills.

Another intermittant problem with this equipment was that men were being paid either bonus or flat-rate money, but not both, then the machine might inexplicably issue a tax refund, as if by way of recompense. This happened to Chargeman Dando, who informed the office he was on his way over and wanted the matter dealt with straightaway. With this done, Dando, the celebrated 'A' shop fitter, who had gone to America with the locomotive *King George V* in 1927, concluded with 'call this automation, I calls it all-to-buggery'.

The Powers-Samas computer was delivered in 1956 to begin running under local conditions. The computer section would be staffed, more or less, from the old paybill machine section and all clerks were to be trained in turn. The new machinery was to do the work in a fraction of the time, but initially, with only the paybills to do, there would be just six operators. Liz said:

Mr Sargeant got us together and assured us how much easier our working lives would become, but at first it was hell. The punchcards were stacked in the computer's magazine but would not be processed if the holes (now called encoded data) were slightly out of line or if the edges of the cards were worn. We had to work overtime to get the cards finished and sent on to the tabulators. We all wished we still had the Hollerith system.

Mr Sargeant came over to run the new computer room. Jeanette Clark was his secretary, Jack Parker was section chief and Gladys Ackrill was the senior female. Some of the others that Liz remembers in that first computer section were Charlie Kimber, who came up from Keynsham, George Brunger, from the wages office, Dennis Vance, Sheila Keen, Tom Fisher and Reg Sumbler. Liz Bartlett left the railway in early 1961, by which time Frank Maslin had taken over as section chief.

The publicity said that 'in early 1957 the computer took over the massive task of complete CME Dept paybill production. Shortly afterwards, all the department's accounting was fully computerized'. According to the *Western Region* staff magazine, 'The machine rented from Powers-Samas reduced the amount of staff working on paybills from 100 to sixty with a saving of £10,000'. George Petfield was employed on the non-automated areas of the paybill production in the years leading up to this. He confirms the vast difference electronic accounting made to the workload.

5

PAYDAY

The story of how the money for wages arrived at the Works was thought worthy of space in the *GWR Magazine* on occasions. Presumably, the writers were given full access to observe the proceedings and quote official statistics, but they were never meant to be a definitive study or historical record. Written in the days when such quaint and timeless rituals were not recorded for posterity, as, unlike nowadays, there was no reason to suspect progress would soon change them for something less interesting.

Every Friday morning (Thursday from some time after 1941) a Mercury tractor from internal transport left the Works hauling a steel and iron-framed box mounted on a chassis. It was bound for Lloyds Bank in Regent Street about three-quarters of a mile away, to collect the wages for the workers within the factory. At the bank, the money was ready to be transported in canvas bags and strong boxes. It was important that exactly the right number of notes and coins of each denomination were received. This was achieved by sending a coin analysis up to the bank earlier in the week. The Works' cashier or a deputy arrived at the bank independently at 9 a.m. to oversee the loading of the money and to sign and exchange the paperwork. Men from the Works' security were present during the loading and no doubt the local bobby was about too. Together with its commitment to other businesses, one can imagine the frenzy of activity at the bank each payday.

The withdrawal was the net earnings for all the weekly-paid men: the manual workers (wages grades); the office/supervisory workers (staff grades); as well as the Swindon footplatemen and shed grades, who came under the Motive Power Superintendents Department, a subdivision of the CME Dept. About 11,500 were based at the Works in the mid-1930s, of whom about 60 per cent were on the loco side. The Works' population increased the following decade and went down again in the 1950s. Just as during the period of this study conflicting figures have been published about how many employees were at the Works at one time, so too is only vague reference found, for publicity purposes, as to how much money left the bank each week. According to the GWR's published figures, the total wages bill for the CME Dept in 1935 was £6.6 million and £8.8 million in 1941. Something over 25 per cent of the CME's wage bill was paid out at Swindon Works. Therefore, the actual amount of cash, after stoppages, leaving Lloyds Bank each week must have been around £25,000 in 1935. The amount for 1941 works out at around £35,000, but this is contradicted by the *GWR Magazine* of the period, which claimed 'about a ton of money, sometimes close on £50,000, left the bank' each Friday. So it is possible that the contradictory 1941 figures were before and after the considerable overtime payments. The report also makes the point that the majority of the money made up the wages of those actually producing the work.

Once loaded, the petrol-driven tractor, which was licensed to run on the public road, would slowly tow the load down Bridge Street. Lloyds Bank was at the near end of Regent Street on

Regent Street from Bridge Street with Lloyds Bank on the right. The men in the picture suggest it was either lunchtime or a Saturday. (Author's collection)

the corner where it crossed the old Wilts & Berks Canal, now disused, and, at that point, filled in. There were two riders: the driver and another man in an elevated position 'riding shotgun', as the locals would say. They turned left onto Faringdon Road and through the GWR estate, passing the Mechanics Institute on the left in Emlyn Square. Alfie, the watchman on the old gasworks' gate, whose surname is forgotten, told George that he used to ride shotgun on the 'pay run'. When asked if he was ever worried about being held up, he said, 'look, I was shot at all across North Africa. If they wants the money they can have it'.

In the early 1940s, with the increasing volume of road traffic, a one-way system was introduced on some roads in the town centre. The pay wagon then suffered the indignity of a long detour up around the Town Hall and back down Commercial Road and Milton Road to reach the GW cottage estate. Bank and railway officials motored back to the Works ahead of the pay wagon. They did not escort the payload, one at each end as seen in the photograph, opposite, until the late 1940s or '50s. Men of the Works' security (watchmen) were not now flanking the procession, as they had done in times gone by, but conspicuously watching the proceedings at a distance – men like a young Bert Stratford, a tall, friendly figure, whom everyone came to know, especially in later years, as a senior watchman and guide escorting groups of visitors around the Works. Enid Hogden (*née* Warren) occasionally rode on the pay run between 1944–48, probably deputising when the regular person was unavailable. She remembers the tractor moved at walking pace, and amazingly Enid does not recall any additional security staff at that time. At the bottom of Emlyn Square, the tractor would turn left and then almost immediately right, with the articulating transport being narrow enough to pass easily in through the double doors of the Bristol Street entrance to the Works. When motor escorts were later used, they were left outside and the occupants followed on foot. The doors were then closed behind them and locked by the gatekeepers until the dinner break. In the mid-1950s, Dave Viveash worked in Dunn & Co., the hat shop, before going 'inside'. He said, 'we always watched the pay wagon go past the shop on Thursday mornings, pulling the red trailer. In the pub later, the lads would speculate on the chances of stealing the money and getting away with it'.

The Pay Wagon returning from the bank to the Works in the 1950s. There was mild panic in the town on one occasion when a vehicle got between the wagon and an accompanying car.

The Pay Wagon tractor was regularly driven by Clem Manning at this time. A second man, a labourer, was chained to his seat and instructed to pull the handbrake if the tractor ran away on a slope. (BR National Railway Museum)

At the far end of the tunnel under the mainline, this main route into the loco works, which was also a fire engine route, took a left turn up a slope. Here the tractor came into its own again and was the other reason for using this sluggish transporter, the Works' alternative to the Scammell 'mechanical horse'. At the top of the slope the vehicles turned right, past the door into the East time office and the progess office. Then they passed No.3 Accounts and the Outdoor Machinery Depot, to stop outside the cash office. This route was well known to visitors then and is still there today, open to the public. This, the main office building for the Works, was known as the Chief Mechanical Engineers block.

The iron money box that was used in the later days of the GWR was still sitting in the old iron foundry when the Works finally closed in 1986 and still had *GWR* painted on either side. It was considered as an exhibit for the Railway Museum but had rusted beyond restoration. The rare photographs of the pay wagon show there were at least two different types of money boxes used since the early 1900s. The pay wagon had been drawn by a Shire horse, possibly up until 1938 – no doubt this was where the nickname 'money hearse' originated. In earlier times the total sum of the money would have been less, but gold sovereigns and half sovereigns, not banknotes, were carried. So I hope the Edwardians attached more horse power to get the load up the steep slope. This was a time when horses were still being used around the factory for pulling carts and shunting wagons, and here again they were superseded by Fordson tractors in the 1930s. After nationalisation, private security vans would deliver the money via the main gate in Rodbourne Road (always referred to as Rodbourne Lane by the railway and consequently everyone else) because the main tunnel entrance was too narrow and had restricted headroom. The gates would be locked until the money was safely unloaded, with the Works' security staff in attendance and accompanied by Alsatians.

The contents of the pay wagon were manhandled into the cash office and the doors locked. The cash office was not to be confused with the wages offices, where the information for the paybills was compiled. Watchmen stood guard outside until the money was distributed to the shops and departments. Unlike the other much larger offices, the day-to-day routine here is less well known – the main function was the actual make up of individual wages on payday.

However, on other days, the small partitioned area at one end of the building was the only part occupied. The chief cashier, his assistant and a couple clerks were resident in the cash office. The staff here dispensed wages at other times in exceptional circumstances, and they handled financial transactions between the staff, the Works and the bank.

Enid Hogden started work in the cash office at the age of sixteen. She had just done six months as an office junior in '22 Accounts' and would not become a clerk proper for another two years. Ernest Habgood was chief cashier in the 1930s but by the time Enid arrived in 1942 George Eynon was in charge. It is thought that Mr Eynon had been the clerk in charge of the GWR Savings Bank some time after Mr Tidball retired in 1932. He remained in the cash office throughout the 1940s and '50s, although George Petfield thinks the senior clerk Isaac Carter took over for a period in that time. Enid noted that Mr Eynon was a meticulous man. She said that 'Mr Mainwaring in *Dad's Army* had a very similar manner to our chief cashier but he was a nice man.' Cyril Davis was the assistant cashier and clerks Joan Thatcher, Phyllis Peddle, Beryl Breakspear and Jean Moses were all in the office at various times during Enid's six years there. When Enid left and moved to the South Coast, she found the wages in similar work a lot lower than in the Western. She said: 'I nearly had to take a job with the Southern Railway' (as it continued to be called, despite nationalisation). When contacting old Swindon colleagues recently, Enid found everyone saying, 'oh yes I remember you, you were the senior clerk in the cash office'. 'Fancy that, sixty years later I find out I was in charge,' she said

After 1952, when the loco and carriage wages offices merged, they had enough staff of their own for 'cash office makeup' as it was referred to (there were 115 wages' staff at Swindon at that time). Because paybill production time had been cut since before the war with the introduction of new machinery, wages' staff was available on payday, where previously staff from elsewhere in accounts were borrowed. Dozens of men and women clerks, mainly from the lower grades, were brought in to makeup and pack the individual wages. Enid said that a senior clerk from the General Managers Accounts was present. He had arrived earlier by train to oversee proceedings and deal with other matters that might have arisen between the two departments. She said, 'I was sometimes sent up to the bank with the pay wagon and at that time there were just three of us: the tractor driver, myself and the man from Paddington.' His weekly visit to the cash office ceased quite early on, possibly due to reorganisation in 1948.

The shops knew it was no good sending their office boy along to the cash office on an errand that day, as it was very unlikely he would be seen. Staff were allocated table numbers and worked in pairs, calculating the total amount of cash required for each batch of earnings in the correct denominations, and drawing this from the cashier. The cashier and yet more clerks were busy breaking down the money, receiving the requisition slips and dispensing the money through one of the three hatches in the partition. Each clerk was given a particular type of coin to dispense. Barbara Carter was in charge of the threepenny bits on her visits to the cash office. On the makeup side, George Petfield remembers being sent down for a trial run to see how it was done, before making up the wages for real the following week. He said, 'You had to have your wits about you to keep up with the others. Wages were often made up in blocks of thirty-eight, but I cannot now remember why.' Clerks worked from summary sheets, which listed the net totals against workers' names and pay numbers. It is possible these sheets held thirty-eight entries. George remembers Clerk Ted Scott working near him when Ted kept counting one bundle of 100 £1 notes and making it £101. With a witness, they accepted that there was indeed an error. They also noticed two notes had the same serial number (this was in the days when £1 was a good proportion of a person's wage). The whole roll had to be returned to Lloyds Bank.

The notes and coins were further broken down into individual net wages by the 'maker-up'. The money was then placed around a circular wooden tray to his or her left, wrapped in the payslip. The tray was turned clockwise on a central spindle. As more amounts were added, another person checked each wage and put it into the correct pay tin or envelope. The checker took longer than the maker-up, so the tray filled up until it held about twenty-five

Pam Whitworth (left) and another clerk making up pay packets in 1956/57. (BR National Railway Museum)

Mr Eynon, the chief cashier, watches as a new clerk counts out money to Dick Minihane. Dick would have been one of the clerks sent down to make up the wages. (BR National Railway Museum)

amounts. Then the maker-up could go around and load the packed wages into strongboxes. A photograph of the cash office taken in 1911 shows that this procedure was the same as George remembers it in the late 1940s, although the old revolving trays did go shortly afterwards. The pay tins were about 2in diameter by 1¼in high. They had the recipient's number painted or stamped on the push-fitting lid. Care had to be taken not to get notes caught between the top of the tin and the underside of the lid, which could then sometimes jam. New notes presented other problems by sticking together and causing vital time to be wasted. The filled tins were placed in the shallow boxes in numerical order and padlocked when full. Mr Richards of the accounts machine room had said that as early as the 1930s counting money by hand and packing it into tins was out of date. He said that 'machinery was now available that dispensed correct sums of money at the push of a button'.

Staff grades had always received their money in paper packets and shop workers pay was packed in individual tins. In the late 1940s, when £5 notes started to be included, they did away with the tins in favour of a buff-coloured envelope and later a cellophane packet. The envelopes were much better to handle. They had the person's name and pay number printed on them and you were told to check your wages before opening the packet, which was not easy. The LMS Railway at Derby was using envelopes with transparent windows by the mid-1930s, but it is unclear whether this included the shop floor. If a discrepancy was found, and the recipient could show beyond reasonable doubt that he or she had been short-changed, according to the payslip, it was the policy to call in the police. It was no doubt a reflection of the times, that although there were a lot of people handling a lot of money, George only heard of this happening once and even then no one was ever suspected of dishonesty.

The designated shop labourer would go to the cash office and collect the pay for the shop. He would lift the boxes containing the pay tins onto one or a pair of sack trucks, and with a pay clerk walk back to his workshop. In some cases this was some distance from the shop, but I have never heard of any incidents which breached security.

As with the making up of the wages, clerks from elsewhere in accounts were borrowed to help with the paying out – even then there was not enough clerks to pay out in every workshop. All the female clerks I have spoken to went out to assist with the payout at various times. It is thought that this was done by men only before the war. Jack Fleetwood said:

> The payout of the wages in the workshop was mockingly referred to as 'the ceremony'. The pay table had been brought out into the shop and assembled, ready for paying out the wages. The wages arrived at the shop with the minders, where they rendezvous with the shop clerk who was waiting to assist the pay clerk. Some men were already lined up, waiting. The pay clerk unlocked the tin boxes but did not touch the pay tins. The foreman appeared at the top of the office steps and looked at his watch. If he was slightly early or he sensed any impatience, he would disappear into his office again before proceeding down to the pay table. Workmen would start to shuffle their feet and the foreman looked at his watch again, waited thirty seconds, and then with a nod of his head the clerks would start paying out the wages. The men were, by now, all lined up in number order. The office boys were the first to slap their paychecks on the polished brass surface. The shop clerk called out the number on the check and the pay clerk ticked the sheet and issued the tin. The check was then sent down the slide into a round tin under the table.

The pay clerk had to certify the paybill sheet so it could be seen by whom each man was paid. After all the attention and care spent on producing the correct payments, the payout appeared to be very hastily done so as to not take any more than five minutes of work time. Men could be seen standing around tapping the upturned tins or sometimes poking a screwdriver in to release the coins and notes before dropping the tin into a basket. Harry Bartlett remembers 'Grabber Greening', of '15' shop, struggling with the pay tin because he had bad arthritus in his hands. Jack said:

The shop and wages clerks 'paying out' in one of the workshops with the foreman in attendance. (BR National Railway Museum)

In the earlier days if the hooter finished blowing before all the men were paid, they would have to wait until the afternoon, which meant a nice little stroll to the cash office where the staff were anything but pleased with the interruption. The following week the foreman would not leave it quite so late, but it was difficult to get the last man away before the hooter blew.

Newcomers were paid their anticipated wage at the end of the first week, with any adjustments being made the following week. If a man was not happy with the amount he received, he explained the problem to the shop clerk. If the clerk could not settle the matter then, and only then, could the man speak to the relevant wages clerk. At the close of the payout, unclaimed wages had to be balanced by the pay clerk with the amounts outstanding on the paybill sheets and with the unissued pay checks. The pay clerk would then make his way back to the cash office with the locked tin containing the paychecks, the pay sheets and any unclaimed pay. This was then enveloped or boxed if not already done and entries written in the 'unclaimed wages register'.

George Petfield remembers that following a severe fire in the nearby oxygen plant, he assisted the paying out in the 'P1' shop, where loco boilers and their fittings were steam tested. Whole sections of the roof were covered by tarpaulin. This was January 1945 when George was a junior clerk. With the shopmen paid, the wages staff could deal with the salaried staff during the afternoon. In pairs, wages and other clerks delivered their money to them personally in the offices and shops. The strongboxes, fitted with dividers, could hold dozens of the lighter wage packets, instead of tins, and be easily carried around by hand. George said that one pair of clerks went off to pay the carriage works' salaried staff, another to pay the CME personal staff and the third pair dealt with the accounts staff, and so on.

Outstation staff would collect their wages from the Works at the end of the week, the following Monday morning or when they could, depending on their travel arrangements. Men on nights collected their wages from the weigh house office or the west end of 'A' shop on the loco side, depending on where they worked. On the carriage side they went to the carriage stamping (forging) shop. The running shed men on nights collected their pay from the machine room office where the paybills were prepared and printed. A worker unable to collect could nominate another to receive his pay check and wages. If a person lived near someone 'on the club' (out sick), they could, if requested, go to the invalid's foreman or office chief, collect an order form and sign and withdraw the wages on his behalf.

Local businesses were all geared up for the extra Friday trade. Jack Fleetwood said:

> Knees, the newsagent and tobacconist just across the road from the works' tunnel entrance, had a problem when pay increased sufficiently because men would rush into the shop with a £5 note and ask for five or ten woodbines. The change soon ran out, so the proprietor began lining up the cigarettes together with the right change for a £5 note on the back shelf, ready for the dinner-time rush. This transaction also allowed the workmen to sort out how much change to put into their pocket before handing over the money to their wives.

Jack never actually saw a wife meet her husband at the factory gates and take his wages, but he did see the Roman Catholic priest outside during Friday's dinner time, waiting for recompense from the Irishman if he had not been seen at mass the previous week. Local children, too, could often be seen waiting to collect their 'Friday penny' from their father.

The iron body of the later pay wagon in the Works in the 1980s. (B. Harber)

6

WORKSHOPS

GWR supporters boast that, at Swindon Works, basic and raw materials such as hard and softwoods, iron and steel, oil, fabrics, leather, water and power went in, and locomotives, carriages and wagons came out. This was, at first glance, the way it appeared. Jack Fleetwood was in the foundry all his working life. He told me that:

> … with its furnaces, Swindon could sort and recycle all the company's scrap iron (with or without additional pig iron and coke) and other ferrous metals, as well as some alloys. And it seemed as though they were self-sufficient. Recycled ingots were analysed in the laboratory, then returned to the furnace with additional metals to produce the required composition.

According to the company's figures, the iron foundry produced between 9,000 and 10,000 tons of castings annually in the 1930s, with approximately 1,700 tons of non-ferrous castings from the brass foundry. There was no steel foundry on site, so wheels, carbon steel ingots and billets, steel bar and plate were brought in to be tested and inspected, and either hammered, drop forged and stamped, pressed or rolled, then machined and heat treated.

In peacetime Swindon received a large amount of its timber from abroad. It arrived mainly through the docks at Cardiff or London then by barge to Brentford; it was examined by the company's inspector before being accepted. Rock elm and hickory came from North America, so did yellow pine which, together with New Zealand pine, was used for making wooden patterns. Oak came in from Poland, pine from Canada, mahogany from Borneo and West Africa and teak for carriage building came from Burma. Usually purchased as logs and trees, it was sawn and artificially seasoned in the Saw Mill and Timber Drying Shed then cut to manageable sizes and sent out to the shops. Most woodworking shops on the carriage side had their own saw mill and could cut the timber down further for their own requirements, sometimes it was received from the supplier as ready-cut boards. One of the few woods used at Swindon for its engineering qualities was lignum vitae, a wood so dense it won't float; they used it to make brake blocks, bearings, shafts and pulley sheaves. Mansell wood wheels had been used extensively for carriages (with steel tyres and bosses) but this practice had ceased by the 1930s. The wooden segments were reclaimed and lined the floors in some areas of the carriage shops. Hardwood blocks, including lignum vitae, were kept in the guard's van of a train along with the jack, so as to secure a temporary repair to axleboxes, excluding the locomotive, where the whitemetal bearing had broken down.

Eight luxury saloon coaches were outshopped in 1931/32 for the Plymouth Boat Train services, with interiors designed and executed by specialist coach builders. As an indication of the annual output of rolling stock, the *GWR Magazine* figures for 1933 were 134 mainline or suburban coaches built, excluding specialist vehicles, such as Post Office vans and brake vans. More than a

Forming a helical spring on a Greenwood & Batley spring coiling machine. (BR National Railway Museum)

third of the existing passenger carriages were still lit by gas at this time. The number of wagons constructed that year was 1,392. The following year an increase in revenue allowed the company to replace and increase its rolling stock considerably. In 1934 they built a total of 246 coaches and 2,470 wagons. They also took possession of 5,000 20-ton mineral wagons built outside. The wagon works, like other departments, sometimes subcontracted orders because they could not handle the work at the time. They would have had to buy in specialised work, for instance the new glass-lined milk tanks which were fitted onto six-wheeled underframes. Two new sets of coaches for the *Cornish Riviera Limited* were built and went into service in 1935, the company's centenary year.

Just after the Second World War, Swindon produced the first track relaying cranes, designed by Ken Webb, in the drawing office. From the 1930s to '50s the carriage bodymaking and frame-building materials changed from mainly wood to mainly steel, but still a lot of timber went into wagon and nonpassenger vehicle bodies. By 1930 galvanised steel panels were fitted to all new carriage stock and to those coming in for overhaul. They were very durable and improved the fireproofing. Horsehair was a valuable commodity, so it was removed from old seats and recycled. It was put through a carding machine over by the carpenter's shop. The machine, operated in the 1950s by Jack Huckin, pulled the hair apart or combed it, then it was washed. It was then bagged up and sent over to the trimmers in '19A' shop for re-use. Those little pictures that were in every compartment on the train were all made in the carriage works with the help of artists and photographers. As well as their contribution to railway carriages, carpenters and cabinet makers produced station furniture, trolleys, platform barrows, sack trucks, ticket and label racks, and fixtures and fittings needed around the factory. No doubt, the check boards used for determining the men's attendance had been made 'inside', as well as the wood and marble Roll of Honour plaques. Upholstery for coaches and furniture was done in the trimming shop, along with a range of leather products, such as tablet pouches (for single-line working), despatch bags and straps of every description.

Besides the overhaul of locomotives at planned time or mileage intervals, the Works built between 100 and 150 new or reconstructed locomotives per annum in the 1930s. They

The iron foundry showing a 20-ton travelling crane. Five-ton swivelling jib cranes and core barrels are seen in the foreground. (BR National Railway Museum)

Pouring molten high-grade iron for a cylinder casting in the iron foundry. The foreman in the trilby hat is Charlie Webb. (BR National Railway Museum)

A set of loco driving wheels mounted in a quartering machine. The opposing crank pins are being machined to achieve the exact position 90° apart. (BR National Railway Museum)

received some batches of smaller classes from private builders and disposed of the displaced engines by cutting up or occasionally selling them. Most repairs to locos, carriages and wagons between planned overhauls were done at the company's smaller works and depots. Apart from supplying motive power and stock for the traffic department, Swindon produced and repaired an impressive range of other items for the GWR, such as outstation pumping and hydraulic machinery, sheet metal fabrications, patterns, track chairs, platform ticket issuing machines, merchandise containers, different types of road vehicle bodies, electric motors for overhead crane mechanisms and even artificial limbs. Bells were also cast on the premises. Jack said:

> Those we cast in the foundry were made of silver bell metal, an alloy of eighty parts copper and ten parts tin, which was expensive to manufacture. We made bells for the company's shipping, for fitting to traversing tables and to dock shunting engines. We made smaller bells for signalling equipment and the A.T.C. boxes in loco cabs. If it was a matter of replacing a part that could be cast, we did it. If a large steam hammer or press developed a crack in its frame, a mould was made of the part and a new piece, sometimes weighing several tons, was made. If a roll needed replacing in the rolling mills we would cast a replacement. We also made some of our own moulding boxes as well.

Not all the company's castings were produced here though. The engineering department made the lineside signs and nameboards displayed around the system. The official line was that Swindon only cast larger batches of such things, on account of the cost.

Signal and train lamps were made or repaired in the Works but handlamps were supplied by an outside firm, as were enginemen's steel (Grimsby) boxes. Some train lighting and other electrical equipment was also brought in. The Works' water-softening plant and oxygen plant were built and subsequently enlarged by specialist companies – the latter a German company. Clocks used in the Works were made by well-known makers but repaired on site in a workshop next to Foreman Bill Holland's office, above 'O' shop. As was often the case, the 'O' shop offices were above the shop's tool store.

Zeiss alignment equipment checks the centre line of re-bored cylinders, with the distance from the horn ways in the frame. The purpose made barrow for transporting this equipment is on the right. (BR National Railway Museum)

Not only could oil be blended and used oil cleaned and refined, the oil works could also produce coolant and hand soap. Paint, putty, grease, bricks, rope, wire, cable, chains, nuts, bolts and rivets were also produced 'inside' but woodscrews and glass were among the 'goods inwards'. Contracts were let and orders placed by the Stores Department – Supplies and Contracts section, the receiving department being debited with the cost. The ten tons of soap powder used each year in the company's laundry was also made up on the premises. Candles were produced from tallow somewhere on the carriage body side. One of the biggest areas of expenditure was stationery and office expendables, and although much of it was marked with the company initials, the factory relied on the specialist suppliers.

The diversity of manufacturing skills practised in one works was impressive – some might say excessive and outdated. It was not always cost-effective to make even those components within their capability. It was the job of the assistant CME to investigate, with the help of the Accounts Department, the cost of manufacture against the cost from a contractor. Mr Gardner, when assistant chief accountant to the CME, said that his department covered work being done for other departments, private firms and other railway companies, and this tends to confront the other myth – that Swindon looked after itself alone. Jack said that 'we did do some work for the signal works. The people at Reading did tend to be very particular about the standard of the workmanship they required of us'.

Cranes, pumps, scales and pressure gauges were brought in. The Works usually looked after any calibration and repair. A policy of continuous renewal ensured such things did not become outdated. Contractors for the manufacturers were responsible for repairs, testing and regulation of the weighbridge, all weighing machines in the Works, as well as the balancing machinery of the locomotive weightable. Air compressors for operating tools, used by the engineering department to break up foundations, were partially maintained by the CME Dept. Any defective tools or hose pipes used with compressed air were, if they could not be repaired on site, either sent back to the makers or to Swindon, depending on prior arrangement. Micrometers, vernier calipers and other measuring instruments were all made outside. Custom-made optical alignment gauges, used for locomotive horn block and cylinder alignment (the only railway company to use this method according to one of the fellows that worked with it) were purchased from the German company Zeiss in the early 1930s. Machine tools used in the factory came predominantly from makers in the Midlands and Northern England, but many of the cutting tools and hand tools were homemade. Machine tools had been made in the factory many years before and two cylinder borers of 1865 and 1881 were still going strong, with the addition of electric motors in place of the old overhead counter-shafting and belt drives, until the end of steam on the Western. Engineering tool rooms would normally make their own jigs, and perhaps gauges, but not usually drills, taps, dies, milling cutters and reamers. Their manufacture was more specialised, but Swindon made the lot, and made them by the advanced method of grinding the cutting surfaces of hardened blanks. The tool room was the showpiece of any engineering works. Here there were 100 machine tools and 140 skilled tool and gauge makers. Dozens of types of chains and lifting tackle were made 'inside', therefore they also had to produce the stores' catalogues that went with them. Some constructional work at Swindon, and throughout the department, was done by contractors under the supervision of the chief (civil) engineer. The company's engineering handbook stipulated that iron and steel brought in for such construction conform to British Standard Specification No.153 – dictating that a high minimum quality of steel was required – and where practical, all materials be of British manufacture.

The manufacturing capabilities of the railway factory were only realised outside when they were required to undertake orders for the Ministry of (War) production, particularly during the years 1941–44. Much of the work for the war effort was very different to the type of mechanical and timber work they were used to, and tested their capacity, skill and resourcefulness. Not only did the Works satisfactorily complete all that was asked of them, they took on work that could not be done elsewhere and usually delivered ahead of time. The loco works' manager during the war, Mr Cook, was awarded an OBE in 1946 for organising the war work undertaken here during his term of office.

Before an order was undertaken, the availability of materials sufficient to complete the work had to be ascertained from the stores department. It was important that work would proceed simultaneously in the various workshops and that all the main component parts came together without holdups. Timber for coach bodies was sawn from logs in the saw mill and further trimmed using a milling machine. The shells were assembled of wood, usually oak and steel members, on their own steel underframe. Thin (16-standard wire gauge, equal to $\frac{1}{64}$in or 1.6mm) steel outer sheets were sheared to shape, after being marked out by machine, then another machine punched in the holes. Wheels and axles were pressed together and machined in their own shop, then sent to '15' shop. Here a gang of about fouteen men did the bogie erecting. Ever greater use was being made of jigs and templates to produce bogies by pressed steel construction. The bogies and underframes (from '13a' shop) were assembled and steam heating pipes fitted, together with the brakegear and drawgear, from the carriage smiths' shop. The complete underframes then went to the body shop where the coach bodies were lifted onto them. Coach finishers fitted all the furnishings and windows. The internal doors, seat frames, panelling and luggage racks came in for fitting from the finishing and polishing shop. Trimmers laid linoleum, rugs and finished the upholstery, and all internal surfaces were cleaned and polished. Finally, the vehicles went by electric traverser to '24' shop to be painted, varnished and lettered. The electrical equipment was also fitted at this stage. There were a total of thirty-four carriage painters. Each coach received three coats of paint and three of varnish, which took seven days to complete.

The '15' shop was the largest C&W workshop, with about 800 men employed, the majority of whom were fitters. The underframes of wagons were constructed in '13' shop. As with carriages, the frames were erected using parts made in the smiths, wheel, machine and fitting shops. The two solebar members were fixed in a jig to secure the wheelbase, then such things as axleguards, spring shoes, transoms, buffer trimmers, stanchions and headstocks were rivetted or bolted to them. The whole frame was then squared up and rivetted to an underframe. Next,

Right: Arthur Myers, a foreman of the carriage side. Mr Myers retired in 1949 after fifty-one years 'inside'. (R. Myers)

Below: Hydraulically lifting a bogie up to a carriage from below floor level in '19C' shop. (BR National Railway Museum)

Moving carriage wheels and bogies using a 7.5-ton Wharton electric crane, which took its power from overhead lines. (BR National Railway Museum)

it was lifted by electric hoist for wheels, axleboxes, tie rods, drawgear, buffers and brakework, to be fitted then painted with red lead before the body was added. Doug Webb worked in '13' shop from the late 1940s onward:

> I worked with chargeman wagon plater Mervyn Iles to start with. Mr Jordan was our foreman and Mr Dobson was the wagon builders' chief foreman. It was very noisy there, as much of the assembly was done by riveting. As a fitters mate, I would take components over the loco side for grinding or heat rivets in a nozzle hand forge.

No one else liked going up ladders, so Doug would spend a lot of time changing pulley blocks that were suspended from swinging jibs. While he was there, a very sophisticated scissor riveting machine was purchased for '13' shop. It was only then found to be far too heavy for the frame that would support it from above. This expensive piece of equipment sat in a corner of the shop and eventually went for scrap, never having been used.

Wagon bodies and merchandise containers were built in '21' shop, and after the war complete overhaul of standard open wagons was done here too. The latter was carried out on two 600ft sections of track stretching the length of the shop. The wagons, including the underframes, were repaired on a belt system to emerge at the other end completed. In the 1950s the Wagon Works as a whole delivered, on average, 300 wagons per week, including 12-ton open and covered goods wagons, ventilated vans, cattle wagons and brake vans back to traffic. The wagon building weekly capacity was, by 1957, equivalent to 100 13-ton open-top types. They were also busy throughout the decade converting hand-braked vehicles to vacuum-braked..

Most of the workshops were uncoordinated and out of date. Only the buildings that made up 'A' shop appeared to harmonise the different stages of locomotive manufacture

Forming stanchion brackets for ballast wagons by first heating, then pressing. (BR National Railway Museum)

A wagon repair line in '21' shop. (BR National Railway Museum)

Chargeman Drinkwater from 'A' shop on the right with enginemen about to return from a trial trip to Dauntsey, with a small Prairie 2.6.2 tank engine. Presumably this is the same Mr Drinkwater who attended to Mr Churchward, an earlier CME at Swindon, following his well-documented tragic accident in 1933. (R. Clarke)

and overhaul. 'A' shop was divided up into AW wheel section, AM machines, AV boilers and AE erecting bays. At the eastern end of 'A' shop, was the engine test plant, with the wooden 'No.4' dynamometer car alongside. After the extensions to 'A' shop in 1921 to take the larger locomotives, there were enough extra-capacity engine pits, electric traverses and overhead cranes to deal with 400 larger-type engines annually.

In the 1930s overhaul practice was altered from 'strip and rebuild' on the same pit with the same erectors, to a 'sectionalised flow system', usually referred to as 'the circuit'. This was spread over several sections. There were also 'new work' sections and light repairs. In the new work pits, the engine frames, together with the hornblocks, were received from the machine shop. They were set up on jigs, then the boiler, cab, steam fountain and reversing handle were fitted to the frames. Connecting, coupling and piston rods, and other parts that made up the valve gear, had been machined and heat treated in the furnace, then cooled in oil, making them both hard and tough to resist wear and stress. The cylinder block and smokebox saddle castings were machined in the 'W' machine shop using cylinder borers and a radical planing machine respectively. Steel tyres were heated in a special furnace in the shop floor of the wheel section. The wheel was lowered into the hot tyre, which had expanded. As it cooled, the tyre shrank onto it. Lowering the locomotive onto its driving wheels was one of the last jobs to be done.

The most costly locomotives to build in the mid-1930s were the four-cylinder *Castles*, costing around £5,000 each. The boiler/firebox was the most expensive component at slightly more than £1,000. The 4,000-gallon tender cost a further £1,000. Other locomotives in the erecting area had been taken out of service for various types of overhaul, depending on the mileage achieved since the last visit. The locomotives were stripped down and cleaned by hand. The smaller parts were taken to 'the Bosh', a small building next to 'A' shop, for cleaning with pressure hoses and lowering into boiling sodium phosphate. The parts were then inspected and passed to the appropriate shops for renewal or repair.

The control board in Foreman Millard's office. The board shows the progress of locomotives through the 'A' shop circuit. (BR National Railway Museum)

John Brettell finished his apprenticeship in 1946 and started in 'A' shop on Georgie Gardener's gang. They fitted the boiler, valve gear and motion bars. 'Apart from the shop's building and stripping boilers, AE shop was the most undesirable area to get stuck in because it was heavy going,' said John. The stripping pits were where the dirtiest and heaviest work took place and Dave Viveash had expected to start there when his time came in the 1950s. Instead, he was sent to work with Harry Bown and Arthur Iles, aligning the cylinders and horn blocks in the main frames in the early stages of locomotive rebuilding. From here he moved to horn grinding, which was done in conjunction with the optical alignment of the frames, and again the work was relatively light and clean. The Zeiss optical method of lining up the frames had first been used on the German state railways. It considerably reduced the time previously spent on this work and increased the working life of the locomotive's motion parts. Dave's next stop was valve setting with Bob Jarvis. Dave said that 'they thought they were a bit above the other gangs in the shop, but it was not as difficult as they tried to make out.' This was the last procedure carried out before going out to the weigh house for wheel balancing, then trials. George says Ernie Nutty, the senior technical assistant in the 1950s, could listen to a trial locomotive move away and tell what adjustments, if any, were needed to the valve settings. Swindon relied more on an ageing, express passenger fleet of locomotives between the 1930s and '50s, compared to other companies. Consequently, the amount of time spent in the Works or stopped at depots increased, while availability decreased.

Despite the state of the economy in the 1930s and the uncertainty of secure employment, there were improvements for the men. The previous fifty-four hour, six-day week was down to a more reasonable forty-seven or forty-eight hours by starting at 8 a.m. instead of 6 a.m., worked over no more than six turns. Labourers and newcomers to the workshops could only join the NUR or Transport and General Workers' Union (T&GWU). After a period in post they were invited to join a union representing their craft, and that's what many shopmen chose to do. There

Lowering a 4.6.0 Hall Class locomotive onto its driving wheels after overhaul. (BR National Railway Museum)

Chargeman W. Hanks, fitters and enginemen during trials with Star Class 4.6.0 *Princess Louise*. (R. Clarke)

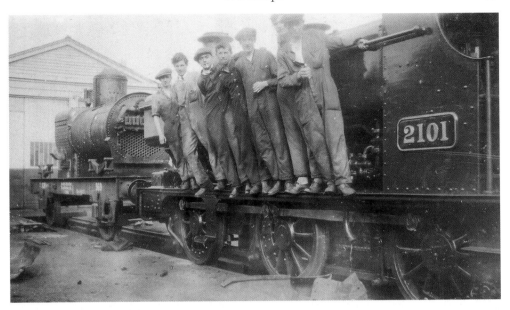

Apprentices outside 'B' shed in 1922. (R. Hatherall, courtesy of R. Clarke)

were about thirty-two different types of crafts represented at railway shopmen's negotiations. Patternmakers, plumbers, foundrymen, coppersmiths, braziers, metalworkers and electricians all had their own societies within the federation of engineering and shipbuilding trades.

The majority of men in the shops were what was known as journeymen: they had successfully completed a recognised apprenticeship in one of the engineering or building trades. Only the eldest son of a skilled man in the service of the GWR might obtain an apprenticeship, the costs of which would be met by the company. It is said that when a boy was born his name could be registered with the company for an apprenticeship place when the time came. The training started on his sixteenth birthday and lasted a full five years with a minimum of two evenings a week at night school. On the 'carriage side' at least, the five years learning fitting and turning were spent as a total of three years on lathes and two on fitting. On the loco side the first two years were spent turning, the next eighteen months on fitting and then the last eighteen months in the erecting shop. Alan Lambourn said, 'despite still learning, we were nevertheless expected to produce'; this together with low wages made them cheap labour. The labour requirements could not be forecast five years ahead, therefore it was in the company's interest to end up with a surplus. Apprentices dismissed at the end of their time were said to be 'going on an improver', if they later returned with a good report, the company would usually take them back. It is often said that most wanted to return to 'the factory' but this was probably because it was the only work available to the tradesman in his home town. After the war the situation changed completely and ex-apprentices were usually retained when their time was up.

With sons following their fathers into the Works in this way, many men had an unbroken family line going back well before the turn of the century. The staff magazine of 1954 recorded the case of chargeman Steward, an erector in 'A' shop. His grandfather came to Swindon in 1852, like so many at that time, from the north of England. His son worked 'inside' all his life and his grandson, along with his two sons, both in 'A' shop, would put in many more years yet. Bert Harber's father, William, had come down from Wolverhampton to be apprenticed in the loco works in the days when the time served was seven years. When Bert started, his father was in AM shop and his three brothers and three uncles were also somewhere in the massive

`Mobile tank removing used coolant from a Churchill plain grinding machine. Another tank would go round and refill the machines. (BR National Railway Museum)

'A' shop. A fourth uncle, Ralph Morkott, a boilermaker, was also there. Only his father-in-law did not work 'inside', having left some years before.

There was a definite divide between workers in the loco and carriage/wagon sides and they rarely ever moved from one side to the other. On the loco side, fitters stripped and assembled components and made sure moving parts worked with each other. Turners were lathe operators who cut internal and external threads, bored out the centre and faced-finished the surfaces of cylindrical work pieces. The gangs of men who assembled the main parts of a steam locomotive were the erectors. There were also welders, electricians, smiths and boilermen but the majority were known generally as either fitters or machinists. Building carriages and wagons also required engineers, as well as tradesmen, such as carpenters, trimmers and coach finishers, and both sides needed painters, joiners, plumbers and riveters. Each profession inevitably became reduced to more basic terms according to the specific work done. He or she might be a 'rubber', 'flatter', 'shingler', 'fettler', 'straightener', 'pressman', 'clothier', 'saw doctor', 'dings separator', 'knocker out', 'holder up', 'hooker on' or any of half-a-hundred other mysterious titles. The labour was divided up into gangs usually consisting of men of the same grade, such as labourers or skilled and semi-skilled. Sometimes they had assistants (apprentices) attached. Individual gangs were known by the surname of their chargeman, who was in charge. I have heard it said that chargemen were not always very agreeable to anyone of lower station, such as labourers and apprentices. Alan Lambourn said that 'some chargemen had been known to clip an apprentice round the ear'. Promotion was usually from within the shop. In Harry Bartlett's experience, most foremen were chosen from the piecework inspectors. A good worker was sometimes overlooked when promotion was being considered because the foreman did not want to lose that man's output. Another unfair practice was that of promoting a union agitator to foreman with a certain knowledge that this would temper his militant ways.

Dave Viveash started his apprenticeship as fitter, turner and erector in March 1956. As usual, his first stop was 'R' (machine) shop. He did not go straight into the 'scraggery'

Handling a white-hot forging for an engine extention frame, under a 4-ton Massey steam hammer. (BR National Railway Museum)

A group of unknown fitters on the 'loco side' taken on 13 March 1937. (B. Harber)

section like Jack Fleetwood. He worked on Reggie Emmon's gang, on special ward 'No.7' combination turret lathes. They turned the larger firebox crown stays and put the threads on them. His first week's pay was about £3 10s 0d. Even at this date, 'R' shop still used some overhead countershafting to drive machinery, and Dave told me (not the first time I have heard it) that some machinery here was salvaged from battleships, possibly German, after the First World War. In the 1950s, the last hour on Friday afternoon became a time for winding down for the week – production stopped, benches were cleaned and machinery was lubricated. An issue of oil and cleaning materials, as well as hand soap, was periodically drawn from the stores.

Most factory photographs were taken before the 1930s, when the Works' foremen wore the bowler hats and this is how they are remembered nowadays. But by the 1940s the younger foremen, especially, were more likely to be seen in the more fashionable trilby. Most larger shops had more than one foreman on the payroll. Swindon's 'A' shop, the largest workshop on the GWR, had four foremen of various grades, one for each of the main sections: erecting, machines, boilers and wheels, as well as a chief foreman. Stan Millard succeeded Mr Plaister as chief 'A' shop foreman in 1934 when he was only in his thirties himself. He remained there until he retired in the mid-1950s and was succeeded by Ernest Simpkins from 'G' shop. Jim Owen, the other long-serving 'A' shop foreman, retired as assistant chief in the early sixties. Mr Millard had been member and contributor of the Swindon Engineering Society and Mr Owen became president of the Foreman's Association. Some chief foremen at Swindon oversaw more than one shop – one was in charge of foundries, the various areas dealing with boilers and another with machine tools. On the carriage side, there were chief foremen for bodymakers, finishers, fitters, painters, sawmills, trimmers and wagon builders. The most senior of foremen were sometimes referred to as superintendent but by the 1930s this title was used more for divisional and outdoor engineers. The term 'the chief' usually meant a reference to the CME himself.

The position of chief foreman was the highest position then attainable by a tradesman, although this had not always been the case. Until the 1920s, apprentices in the loco works, who had shown considerable academic distinction and transferred to the drawing office early in their careers, could go all the way to the top. They may also have become an elected member of the Institution of Mechanical Engineers. All the most senior men in the drawing office in the 1940s and '50s were ex-Swindon apprentices, as indeed was the CME himself, Mr Hawksworth. Apprentices who excelled might still be offered a three-year studentship, a small number of which the directors kindly offered free each year. The object was to raise the general standard of technical training among those who were capable of higher positions in engineering.

Many youngsters in the town wanted to become engine drivers and their fathers would point out that they would not like the shift work. There were only limited opportunities to work on the footplate, so most of those young men settled for work in the factory as long as it was on the loco side. By the 1950s some boys were more interested in aircraft than trains and would apply first to Vickers-Armstrong, where they had an apprentice training school.

Jack started 'inside' when he reached fifteen years of age. As with all new starters, he presented himself at the tunnel office and was taken to the designated shop office by another recently appointed junior. On the carriage side, Harry Bartlett remembers being taken over to '14' shop by Bert Rawlings, the registrar from the C&W time office who also dealt with the new recruits. Until he could start his apprenticeship at the age of sixteen, Jack spent the year in 'R' shop in the 'scraggery'. Here there were about thirty juniors working basic lathes under two chargemen. The automatic machinery was set up by turners acting as tool setters but production was done by the youngsters who also fed the lengths of bar into the lathes. The scraggery was one of the few production areas certified to allow boys to work – another was the 'N' (bolt) shop. Jack said that 'Swindon got through a lot of bolts'. It had been policy never to re-use them on locomotives if they had been drilled to take splitpins, but assuming

A line of Ward 'No.10' combination turret lathes in 'R' machine shop. (BR National Railway Museum)

they were in good condition, they did start re-using them after the war. Jack said that 'nuts and bolts were cheap enough to buy in and that's what most firms did. Not us though, because while the low paid were producing them, we could make them just as cheap'.

One of the smaller lads working in the scraggery might be sent to 'B' shed, where the assembly and dismantling of tenders took place. Alan Lambourn remembers being given a lighted candle which was pressed into a large nut to form a base and being sent inside the tender tank.

> I had to crawl to the narrow front end and fasten nuts and washers onto bolts that were pushed through from the outside. You disturbed a lot of rust in there and if you sneezed and blew out the candle, you were in trouble. I remember too finding small dead fish in the bottom of the tender tank. They once lived in the lineside water tanks that supplied the columns.

Typically, Alan spent some of his apprenticeship on the loco side, learning fitting on machine tool maintenance. In Georgie Marchment's gang they would strip down tool room machinery, replace worn parts and rebuild them. Later he moved on to the 'R' shop 'safety valve gang', which was mainly bench fitting with Tommy Marchment's (George's brother) gang.

Jack's father could not afford the £110 cost of a Premium Apprenticeship for his son, nor could he afford to keep him while Jack repaid the costs of learning a trade. Because of working 'inside' himself on internal transport, Mr Fleetwood senior was classed as semi-skilled and therefore could only manage to secure a semi-skilled position for his boy. Jack was given a choice of work upon reaching sixteen years of age. He could choose between rough painting wagons and buildings, moulding or machining. His father enquired which job paid the most. The moulder got an extra shilling a week on the rate, so Jack started in the brass foundry with chargeman George White. Doug Webb's father was a skilled man, a chargeman wire rope splicer, but he had an older son who became an apprentice boilermaker, leaving Doug to become a labourer. Doug also started in the boiler shop on Rodbourne Road in 1936. The head boiler foreman was a Mr Eburne. Fireboxes had to be drilled, tapped and stayed by pneumatically operated tools suspended with counterbalanced tackle from above. Doug said: 'I started as a "water boy", as the men worked on these and the boiler barrels. I poured water

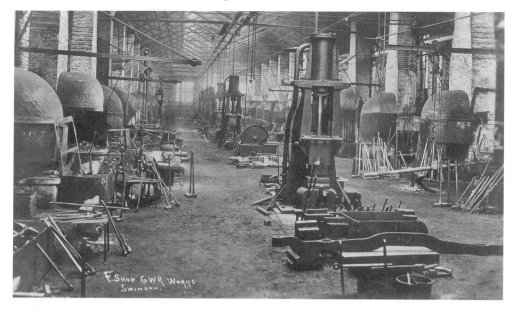

An early photograph by the well-known local photographer Hooper of part of one of the two general smiths' shops. The blacksmiths' forges can be seen either side, and small steam hammers and a circular saw in the middle. (Author's collection)

over the cutting tools to keep them cool'. Some of this was done from the inside, so Doug had to work with a candle and a box of matches signed out of the stores.

Working on steam boilers was very noisy because of the use of hydraulic riveting guns against the heavy plated barrel and box fabrications. These men would soon develop hearing problems, and it is well known locally that a retired Swindonian with indistinct speech and a hearing aid was likely to have been a boilerman. As well as 'V' shop boilermakers, Doug spent time in 'P1' shop, where the completed boilers were taken to have their fittings attached. They were then tested with steam from a master boiler, thus avoiding the need to fire them up in the normal way. A tunnel, through which the boilers were taken, connected the two workshops which were either side of Rodbourne Road. 'The irregular bursts of high-pressure steam soon played havoc with your nerves here too,' Doug said. The men could apply for other types of work in the vicinity. Any vacancies were displayed on the noticeboard. Doug managed to move and was based in the nearby 'tube house' with chargeman Ernie Fisher and assistant Jessie Pettifer. Here, the flue tube ends were machined to fit the tube plates at each end of the boiler. The tubes were stretched at one end and narrowed at the other. 'I still found myself in the boiler shop a lot of the time but the balance (piecework bonus) was better here. Another thing I remember about the tube house was the dust coming down when the rats ran along the pipes overhead'. Doug saw one poor fellow, a 'hooker on', crushed by a boiler when the chains suspending it gave way. He said, 'that was 1937/38, can't remember his name, he lived in Princes Street. The mood in the shop was very subdued for the rest of the day.' A little later Doug saw a friend suffer a nasty injury when some scrap iron fell on his arm in the rolling mills. He decided he had had enough. With his father's blessing, he left the Works in 1939.

Peter Reade was not a local lad but was looking for alternative employment. He had an uncle who lived in Swindon and worked 'inside'. Peter said that 'the idea of working with steam engines seemed exciting to me so Uncle Charlie Pipkin, a C&W upholsterer, got me an application form for the Swindon Factory'. The company preferred newcomers to have an older relative already in their employ who would vouch for them. The rule that only sons

Forging a trailing horn block under a 6-ton Brett drop stamp. (BR National Railway Museum)

and daughters of workers could apply for work in the Western had presumably been relaxed slightly when the need for labour increased. After an interview and a medical, Peter started in 'F' (loco side smiths) shop in 1939, along with some other chaps who were all about his age. The work of the smiths was, by diverse means, to heat steel ingots, blooms and wrought iron, then forge it into shape, usually by hammering. This work was carried out in two unconnected areas: 'F' and 'F2' shops, (between the two were the big steam hammers, 30cwt up to 5-ton capacity, which forged coupling rods, connecting rods and extension frames). Peter said, 'Donald Grant, Bill Tidmarsh, Gordon Glover and myself all trained to be steam hammer drivers. We were each put with a gang of four men working the smaller 10 and 20cwt hammers. As drivers, we set the hammers and controlled the blooms as they were fed in. When we progressed to larger hammers, we forged the con rods and extension frames for locomotives.' Down the sides of the shop were blacksmiths' forges, each with an open tank of water (called a bosh) to cool the blacksmiths' tongs. The steam hammers and furnaces were down the centre of the shop, and halfway down both shops was a large circular saw that was used to cut through hot metal. Other areas in the smiths' shop included stamps or drop hammers, chainmakers, springsmiths and a gas welding section. The other type of heat treatment done by smiths elsewhere was that of normalising, annealing, hardening, quenching and tempering of components and tools. Carefully controlled heating and cooling was usually done to produce the high tensile, toughened, hardened steel and iron needed to resist wear and the stresses of tension and compression. Cutting tools, rope wire, couplings, buffers, tyres, axles, brake blocks and springs were heat treated.

'F' and 'F2' shops were about 33,000sq.ft. The floor was just earth, which was sprayed with water every now and then to keep the dust down, and components were stacked on steel plates. Despite the heat from the forges and furnaces, it could be very cold and draughty in winter, especially for the hammer drivers. There were three foremen in the smiths' shops in Peter's time: Alfred Legge, springsmiths; Frank Mason, smiths; and Mr Titcombe steam hammers and stamps. Herbert Parker was the chief foreman. The men wore leather aprons and

A large locomotive connecting rod is checked with calipers. It has been forged under a 4-ton Massey steam hammer. (BR National Railway Museum)

pads to protect against flying sparks and embers. 'Four of us hammer drivers tried to join the Navy but were turned away for being underage. A lot of the younger men in the smiths' shop, as elsewhere, volunteered and were accepted into the Forces before we found ourselves in a reserved occupation,' said Peter. Later in the war, when they were thinking of putting women on to steam hammers, Peter and the others were asked if they wanted to learn the art of the blacksmith. They jumped at the chance and after three years of 'working on the other side of the anvil' they were able to call themselves skilled tradesmen.

The 'inside mate' got the metal to the right heat. He was the senior striker and earned slightly more. The blacksmith held the work while strikers hammered it alternatively. The smith moved it and turned it, thus controlling the form it took. Most blacksmiths had one or two strikers and some jobs required even more. They had to make all their own tools and were always in demand to make items for use at home (known as foreigners), such as pokers, chisels, axe heads and even iron gates. The foremen were normally very strict but in return for the odd foreigner for themselves, they turned a blind eye to the practice, within reason. The proper work of the loco blacksmith was to fashion cab fittings, such as regulator handles (known as starting handles 'inside') and brake levers. Engine piston rings were also roughed out by the blacksmith before being machined. Con rods, coupling rods and large motion gear were forged with steam and drop hammers. On the carriage side, there were seventy-six skilled smiths in the early 1930s. The only machines they had were two hot saws and nine steam hammers – by 1948 there were 109 C&W smiths. Their work included producing brake systems, fittings for goods containers, as well as numerous tools used in the Works and elsewhere on the railway. A lot of coupling links were also manufactured by the C&W smiths, using a pneumatic 5cwt hammer.

Other men remembered in Peter Reade's shop were 'Spud' Taylor, Frank Ellis, Peter Vizard, Alec Leach, Eric Bradley, Ken Pinnegar and Jim Poole, who came over from the C&W side and was a big union man. A number of people have pointed out, it is not easy recalling names, as many workers were only known by a nickname. Peter joined the AEU, as a lot of the smiths and strikers were members of this union. Their own union, along with several other crafts, had been amalgamated to form the new AEU in 1920. He said: 'To pay my dues, I used to meet a bloke in the pub down by the old Golden Lion Bridge.' The company forbid such transactions to take place in the factory before the 1940s.

Another 'hot shop' was the rolling mills. Doug Webb started working there as a 'puller up' in the late 1930s, when Billy Davis was the foreman. Doug said that 'it was hell in there, very hot and, until you got used to it, very dangerous. I had no choice, as a labourer I could be moved from one shop or area to another'. The puller up got the steel billets and blooms into and out of the furnaces by sliding them along on rollers. Large pieces of white hot metal were slid across the floor which was lined with iron plates. No outsider dared walk through the shop. They used 'Grade C' iron, which was made from assorted scrap, and 'A' and 'B' iron, which came from selected irons melted down. The 'shingler' in the rolling mills used large pairs of forceps to turn white-hot iron under a drop forge. By the 1930s this was believed to be the only place in the country still using this method. One or two shinglers wearing face guards, white smocks, leather aprons and iron boots turned the white-hot mass between hammer blows. A third man controlled the hammer with a lever at the side. After the metal was compressed sufficiently it was slid across the floor and passed quickly through roughing rolls and back through finishing rolls, which squeezed it into a long bar. It was then cut into sections, causing a spectacular show of flying sparks. All this had to be done before the billet cooled too much and hardened. The mills themselves consisted of a 10in and 14in roll, each driven by a stationary steam engine built in the Works in the nineteenth century.

There were no proper (tea) breaks when Jack Fleetwood first started 'inside'. Although this meant that for those who could get away with it, no time was deducted while consuming some refreshment. Like many others, he took in a tea can, some sugar and a tin of condensed milk. Doug remembers cocoa as being more popular than tea in the 1930s. He said:

> If you got caught having a drink in the boiler shop, you were sent home for three days. Some foremen were more sympathetic. If Taffy Thomas, the foreman in the iron foundry, came across anyone having a drink or a crafty draw, he usually said 'that's alright lads', as he lit his own pipe. Then you had the foundry's foreman himself nervously looking out for the loco works' manager. The rest of us still had to watch our backs because the junior foreman Charlie Webb was a 'works man' and did not negotiate over the rules. When you were working and you sensed someone approaching, you kept your head down. If Taffy's shiny shoes came into view, you often found a sweet on the bench after he had gone. Only if people from Paddington were looking round did the CME himself appear, with labourers having previously put in some overtime to get the shop tidy. I occasionally spotted Mr Hawksworth when he was in charge but I never saw the reclusive Mr Collett. Mr Cook came through sometimes and always spoke. He was down to earth. It is surprising how few workers I have spoken with ever saw the chief mechanical engineer.

Nights at Swindon were worked on a rota. Even though there was a small permanent night shift in some shops, others never had a night shift, and with a few it depended on the scale and urgency of the work being undertaken at the time. A few men preferred nights, in which case they could take on extra from those who hated them. When Jack Fleetwood became junior foreman, he continued to give away his nights and was told his enhanced pay included a night allowance, so he must do his share. Jack said: 'During the war, when you went in on the nightshift there was often a freight waiting in the loop at Rodbourne Lane, usually with a 28XX simmering at the front. When you came out in the morning it was often still there.' Even with the odd spell of nights, the factorymen did not envy the shifts worked by the lads at the running shed or on the footplate. Jack said:

> The first thing you did when you arrived at night was to put your sandwiches into a tin box to stop the rats getting them. Because of the reduced light, in wartime we would sprinkle white powder onto cast surfaces to identify rough spots, and until an alternative was found, we used household flour to which the rodents were attracted.

Small stampings sealed in an iron box are pushed into a gas furnace to be case hardened. (BR National Railway Museum)

All GWR land and premises came within the Rats and Mice Act in 1919, and if infested, the company was required to take all necessary steps to exterminate the pests. Swindon men said the only steps taken were the reliance on cats, before poison was used in the 1950s. There were, for many years, two cats in the iron foundry but cats had always refused to stay in the brass foundry, so Jack and his mates caught rats in humane traps. They then tried to gas them but this was a slow process, as the rodents seemed to like coal gas and would push their noses up the pipe. The company handbook offered no suggestions as to methods of eradication, only that 'if necessary the CME Dept should seek the assistance of the Divisional Engineer'.

The taking of snuff or chewing tobacco was very popular in the workshops. The old boys who took snuff turned their white moustaches brown. Until the end of 1939, smoking was strictly prohibited for safety reasons. Jack says he never knew of serious gambling 'inside' or out in the town, but his workshop, like some of the others, had a 'bookies runner', the man who took bets and placed them, on the men's behalf, in the dinner hour. He said, 'When "Walters", the bookmakers "up the lane" [Rodbourne Road], had a lot to pay out, they would often ask the men to accept their winnings in tea or sugar.' The football pools collector was another traditional part of life in the factory. You had to keep in with the 'pools man' in Jack's part of the Works. Then if you had a win he would forget to tell the taxman. The pools man, who took over in the loco wages office in 1954, is still collecting from some of those same people at their homes to this day, said George Petfield.

In the iron foundry, old broken castings and bars of new pig iron were melted in the foundry cupola, a small blast furnace. When the fire in the furnace had burnt up, the blast was gradually increased to raise the temperature sufficient to melt the metal. The molten metal was poured into a hollow shape or mould, which when cooled produced a solidified casting. A sample might also be sent to the laboratory. Jack's job as the moulder was to produce the hollow. The usual way to do this was by 'closed box moulding'. A loose pattern in the shape of the required finished casting was placed in the box of two halves, sometimes more, and packed with sand. The pattern was then carefully removed by separating the box, so it was important

Linen sewers in '9A' shop. (BR National Railway Museum)

that the sand was of the right consistency. The type of sand used varied, depending on the work. 'We used a lot of "green sand" which was black and for some work we mixed horse manure with it, which helped to dispel the hot gases,' said Jack. If the casting was to be hollow or have any cavities, cores would be added at this stage by the 'coremaker'. Channels to let in the molten metal and allow the hot gases to escape were now also added. The top cover was put on and had to be held down to stop the molten metal lifting it. Jack said:

> Locomotive cylinder/saddle blocks were probably the most exacting work we did and required the best quality cast iron. Up to twenty-six separate cores could be used but I never saw "a scrapper". On the other hand, plain scrap was used for loco and carriage brake blocks, the latter known as slippers.

Another method was 'open sand moulding', where the mould was bedded in the foundry floor then covered by a top-part moulding box. This avoided the need for expensive bottom-part moulds, particularly those for bulky irregular castings. Large castings, weighing several tons, took more than two weeks to complete, with all the preparation and the cooling, fettling and cleaning afterwards (fettling involved grinding off any ridge left between the two halves of the moulds). All the moulds had to be ready by early afternoon as this was when the furnaces, which were lit first thing in the morning, would be ready. 'With heavy castings being hoisted around and molten metal splattering unannounced, the foundry was full of hazards, even for the resident workforce. So imagine the amazement one Wednesday afternoon when a woman with a pushchair got separated from the guided tour and came wandering through the shop,' said Jack.

The usual sequence was for castings to go on to the machine shop for various operations and partial assembly, then on to the erecting shops as main component parts. As well as moulders, other grades working in the foundry were dressers, furnacemen, knockers out, cupolamen and ladle runners. Behind the iron foundry was the chair foundry, where semi-skilled men produced track chairs and other castings for the permanent way. The chargeman chair moulder in the

1950s, Harry Johnson, said his forty-three men were the best paid of their grade in the factory. Jack said 'their work was hard and tedious, and the conditions were dirty and cramped'.

In peacetime, women conciliation/wages staff were employed in the CME Dept as office cleaners, charwomen, gatekeepers, carriage cleaners, linen sewers and machinists. At Swindon, women were also employed as stores assistants and laundresses. Women's pay for manual work was about half of what the unskilled workshop man took home, although his working conditions were likely to be a lot tougher, and girls were paid significantly less again. It is not clear whether the wage figures given were for full- or part-time hours. Office cleaners' hours, for instance, are known to have varied considerably. The ladies first entered the Swindon workshops after the First World War, replacing men who had been killed or disabled. They worked with the range of fabrics and wood finishes for carriage interiors and furniture. The utilisation of women was never fully exploited in the C&W Works. Before the war the polishing shop had three sections, one of which was staffed by women and overseen by forewomen Miss Fagin. After 1945 only women worked here. They produced fine finishes on hardwoods by French polishing, staining and laquering. The other areas of the shop floor that women worked in were the trimming shops and sewing room, where as well as carriage upholstery, they made aprons, canvas bags, table clothes, towels, window straps, flags, blinds, axle box pads, cushions, pillows, slips and so on. A purpose-made women's restroom and mess room were provided in 1939 for employees in the sewing and polishing shops.

Princess Elizabeth visited Swindon Works on the afternoon of 15 November 1950 after performing some civic duties in the morning. As had happened when her grandfather visited in 1924, the longest-serving staff members were presented to the royal guest on a tour around selected workshops. The princess was naturally taken around the areas of the carriage shops where the work of female manual workers could be seen. Those who met Her Royal Highness included Miss B.J. Baden, forewoman in charge of the sewing room, who had worked 'inside' for an impressive forty-six years; linen sewer chargewoman Miss M. Webb with thirty-one years; Miss R.M. Woodroffe of the polishing shop with twenty-nine years; and chargewoman French polisher Miss I. Newton with twenty-six years. The Works provided a welfare section for women (and men) by the 1930s; the rest of the company did not get a women's welfare officer until 1941. According to the staff magazine in 1948, the Western Region as a whole employed 8,000 women, half the number it had been in 1943.

The Factory and Workshop Act of 1901 was a parliamentary enactment designed to ensure that manufacturing could be achieved without risk to health and without the exploitation of women and young persons under the age of eighteen. A factory was defined for the purposes of the Act as 'any workshop where power other than just manual labour was in use'. A workshop was defined as 'a place where only manual labour was exercised by way of trade or for other purposes of gain' – the latter applying more to sheds and warehouses of the chief goods managers department. The whole of the company's workshops, whether they belonged to the Engineers, the Signal department or the CME Dept, were thus classified as factories or shops, even if only one person was employed in them.

Works' managers and divisional superintendents in charge of workshop personnel were responsible for seeing that measures were taken to prevent personal injury to those under their control. A current rule book and general appendix giving clear safety instructions was issued to each person, and an abstract of The Factory and Workshop Act, The Workman's Compensation Act and The Notice of Accident Act, 1906, were displayed in every shop which qualified as a 'factory'. The company officials were required to make periodic inspections of workshops under their control to ensure machinery and appliances were maintained in a safe condition and used only for their intended purpose. Men suffering from a disability were not to be employed in positions they could not cope with because such a handicap would expose them to additional danger. Ambulance (first aid) cabinets were supplied to all depots and workshops. They were to be regularly inspected and stocked by a competent person. All the workforce were encouraged to learn first aid and were supplied with basic instruction

One of the castings displayed in the foundry which was produced for the royal visit in 1950. (B. Harber)

booklets. The Act required that a supply of clean water for drinking and washing was supplied where twenty-five or more men were employed. In reality, many men in the shops spoke of limited access to fresh water during the shift, particularly pre-war, unless they were in direct contact with furnaces, fires and steam hammers. Peter Reade remembers being given a drink designed to stop sweating when he first went into the smiths shop in 1939, but soon after, he said, 'that was stopped. Yes we had access to enough drinking water but only really needed it in the hot weather'. To obtain hot water for washing hands and face, some men said they had to drop a piece of hot metal into a bucket of water. District factory inspectors had, on behalf of the Home Office, full powers to examine premises which came under the Act at any time and see that health and safety requirements were being enforced.

Every factory area on the Great Western that employed young persons under the age of sixteen had to obtain a Certificate of Fitness. The loco and carriage works managers would hire a certifying surgeon who would inspect the site and, if appropriate, issue the certificate. For this, certain standards regarding temperature, ventilation, sanitation and illumination had to be met. Since 1939 a policy of changing from gas to electric lighting had been undertaken to comply with the Factory and Workshop Act. Electric lighting installation and maintenance had been the responsibility of the CME since 1924.

The conditions at the Works appear to have fallen short of the requirements of the Act, as many production areas were off limits to boys under sixteen years of age. Apart from the few places on the loco side already mentioned, some boys did work in carriage shops. The large fitting and machine shop was one of them. Basic conditions for the men were not so clearly defined, concentrating more on the procedures once an accident had occurred. Every accident which resulted in an absence from work of three days or more was recorded in the general register and notice sent to the district inspector of factories.

The department would have to provide records of regular treatment to seal walls, floors and ceilings or lime washing. For 3*d*, the men could take a brush and a bucket of whitewash from the medical centre and treat walls at home. 'It made the dark corners lighter if nothing else,' said Jack. The ventilators in Jack's shop were, for the majority of the war, covered with blackout sheets, making conditions very unpleasant at times. These were not picked up by any factory inspector.

7

OTHER WORK

INTERNAL TRANSPORT

A considerable amount of the work of internal transport was moving components between workshops during the different stages of manufacture. There was also all the supplies to be delivered around the site from the various stores and laundry. They would move machine tools into position, ready for them to be bedded in by the bricklayers. This was usually done on weekends to avoid disruption. In total, 1,145 tons of items were transported around the Works each day in the 1950s. Jobs outside the factory included taking coke to the mechanics reading rooms in Gorse Hill and Rodbourne, and to the luggage office under the station. Gordon Turner joined the Transport Department in 1947 as a labourer. His first work was unloading scrap metal going into the foundry furnaces. In the early days, Transport would collect horse manure from the stables at Transfer Goods Depot about a mile east of the Works for use in the foundry. Every year men from the Transport Department worked outstation, digging and loading red sand at Kidderminster, which was also for use in the foundry.

The Transport Depot was next to the 'F2' smiths shop on the loco side. In the 1950s, Gordon remembers:

> There were thirty drivers and twenty to twenty-five labourers. We had thirty-four tractors of various types (they were supplied by the Mercury Truck & Tractor Co. and had been since at least 1938), six petrol/electric mobile cranes, four rigid lorries, four forklift trucks and a large and small loading shovel. Another tractor was kept on the 'carriage side' just for moving batteries between the Battery House and the sidings where they were fitted into coaches.

At that time, the Works undertook an investigation into problems with internal movements of materials by railway wagons. They found that, as well as congestion, wagons were not being used to capacity and far more reliance should be placed on internal road vehicles. Depending on the size and weight of the loads, there were several types of vehicles available to them. Hand carts (or bogies) and mechanical or petrol trolleys with trailers were used for smaller loads. You did not need a license to drive vehicles 'Inside' but you had to be over twenty-one years. Tractors usually hauled 1-ton trailers but larger loads up to 20 tons, such as loco cylinder blocks, and frames could be taken on specially constructed trailers. Bulky loads were also carried in railway wagons and shunted between shops by tractor or by locomotive. Before the 1950s, horses were also used to some extent. Some tractors were fitted with towing plates front and back, and they shunted coaches in and out of '21' and '19' shops. Gordon remembers factory transport men were Harry Stiles, Percy Smart, Derek Johnson and Clem Manning.

Gordon's brothers also worked on the transport – Stan joined in 1950 and Ivan in about 1954. Teddy Rowe was the internal transport foreman in the 1940s and '50s. Reggie Hinton took over in the late 1950s.

THE WATCHMEN

Outsiders coming onto works' land uninvited were usually just young men trying to spot locomotives. However, crossing the busy running lines could be very dangerous with so much activity going on and the authorities took a dim view of it. In those days adults took responsibility for their own actions and expected to face the consequences, without sympathy. So it was probably not the injuries of intruders that concerned the company so much as adverse publicity – perhaps even an inquest and questions that would have to be answered at all levels. Much of the railway works was surrounded by high brick walls but there were places where iron railings formed the boundary and these could be breached, especially with the help of a mate or a wooden box. It was difficult for conspicuous young children not to get noticed with so many workers about but some corners of the railway yards were quite remote.

The duties of the watchmen were of two main types: 1) patrolling the shops and yards between 6 p.m. and 7 a.m. on weekends and public holidays; 2) to act as gatekeepers at the Works' entrances. The premises were divided up into a number of areas to be patrolled; each watchman was responsible for one round each turn of duty. He was to apprehend trespassers and look out for fires; each round took about an hour and had a number of stations which had to be visited. To prove he had covered the rounds as required, each station had a fixed key, which when applied to a clock he carried, recorded the exact times he was there.

At the entrances, the watchmen had to be seen, in order to deter intruders and check suspicious-looking activity. Workers leaving before their normal finishing times were required to present a 'pass out' to the man on the gate, who would endorse it with exact times of leaving and re-entering. Goods, and the accompanying paperwork, arriving at or departing from the Works was dealt with by the watchmen, who also received the mail from the postman. In addition to the watchmen on the gates, others were employed at the various railway crossings, which gave access between the Works and the railway lines running through it. Jack Fleetwood said: 'I remember two distinct types of men employed to maintain security around the Works. Some were overcome with a sense of self-importance in the watchman's uniform, while others were quite agreeable'.

George Petfield told me the story of an unofficial visitor who was spotted at the running shed in the late 1940s by Frank Cottrell. The engine spotter decided to make a run for it through the Works, pursued by the short burly watchman for some considerable distance. The intruder easily kept ahead of Frank but was caught as others joined the chase. In court the villain was fined, and when asked if he had anything to say, said 'I should like to apologise for the distress I have caused to the short fat man who chased me.' The other watchmen who were present with Mr Cottrell ensured the apology passed into works' folklore.

THE LAUNDRY

The company's Central Laundry had been sited in the C&W side at Swindon from 1893 until 1938 when a new building was opened. The laundry's workforce was almost entirely female and presumably always had been, as the *GW Magazine* reported in 1931 that a Mrs Robinson, one of the laundresses, had worked there for thirty-four years. The only man was the foreman, who may have also looked after the machinery. Wicker boxes filled with used laundry came in from the company's hotels, refreshment rooms, sleeping cars and camping coaches. Towels made up the biggest proportion of items dealt with. Linen, blankets, d'oyleys, dusters and

A general view of the new GWR Laundry shortly after opening in 1938. (*GWR Magazine*)

antimacassers were also laundered and starched, then sent back. Thirty-six laundresses were employed before the old laundry closed, when there were five washing machines, four hydro-extractors (driers) and three large ironing machines. The new building was sited close to the station for easier delivery and despatch of consignments. The washing, drying and ironing machinery was of course increased and, in addition, there was now a sewing machine section for repairs. Fifty staff worked in the new laundry, including a resident engineer in charge of the machinery and water-softening plant.

STORES DEPARTMENT

In the early 1930s, Mr Cookson was the superintendent of the Stores Department; when he retired his assistant Mr Boxall took over. Mr Webb and Mr Willis were the assistants to the superintendent, the next title down from assistant superintendent. The other senior stores posts were the storekeepers, chief clerk and inspector of materials. Most, but not all of the storage and distribution of stocks was centralised at Swindon Works because Swindon was the biggest purchaser. The Stores Department was divided up into four main areas: locomotive, carriage and wagon, timber and general stores; each had a storekeeper and an assistant in overall charge and as with the larger workshops, each store had an office run by a chief clerk. Each, except the timber stores, was further divided up into numerous warehouses. The storekeeper was responsible for the orderly storage and handling of stock, as well as for supplying the works, depots, outlying stores, and in the case of the general stores, stations throughout the company. He had to strike a balance between supplying items without holding up production, and holding only sufficient quantities to minimise loss of capital interest and the risks of deterioration or obsolescence. Storage and distribution of coal at the three local coal wharves also came under the control of the Stores Department.

The blending room in the oil and grease works. Below the floor were huge storage tanks.
(BR National Railway Museum)

One of the larger stores in the carriage and wagon works. (*GWR Magazine*)

Goods inwards were purchased from contractors and other departments and sold within the company. Raw materials were randomly tested in the stores test room by the inspector of materials, to ensure they were up to the job. Before stores were received, contracts had to be drawn up, orders placed and accounts kept, and this was done in the department's offices. The stores also dealt with scrap; residual materials were sent back to Swindon where the department received it, reclassified it and sold it. During the war, the CME Dept recycled much of this. According to the *GWR Magazine*, 'Striking economies in the use of all materials have been effected by a variety of special means including modern methods of reclamation and the painstaking salvage of bomb damaged and worn equipment for repair and reuse'. It fell to the Stores Department during this period to find suitable substitutes for scarce items.

The 230 staff in the loco stores handled items ranging from copper boiler plates, heavy iron and steel sections, raw materials in the form of steel blooms, billets and bars for the rolling mill and stamp shops, base metals for the foundry, loco wheels for turning and other semi-manufactured components ... right down to bolts and nuts. They also kept paint, permanent way materials, gas and electrical fittings, crane and turntable parts. Another 176 people worked in the C&W stores. Besides every component for the current rolling stock building programme, they held road vehicle parts, oil and grease and plate-layers materials. The General Stores Department was also based in the factory and had premises across the system. Their function was primarily to supply the Traffic Department with materials and consumable stores. Travelling stores vans were sent out to deliver every type of 'tool for the job', such as lamps, brooms, towels and cleaning materials on a new-for-old basis. The vans were attached to passenger/parcel trains and each of the five vehicles supplied a different area of the system; with them went the attendants, known as 'tallymen'. In addition to the stores vans, a further fleet of vehicles was based at the general stores for the purpose of delivering consumable stores quarterly to something like 1,100 offices, stations and depots.

WORKS FIRE BRIGADE

The brigade consisted of a chief officer, a second officer and twelve firemen who were available for immediate call. There were about six men working full time in the station, maintaining fire appliances and equipment, as well as fighting fires and practising fire drills. Presumably, to comply with the Factory and Workshop Act, auxiliary fire points were situated around the factory where pumps and extinguishers were available. All firemen had to live close by in the GWR estate and had an alarm system between the station and their homes. The part-time firemen worked in the shops, offices and yards. In wartime their number was increased to twenty-four. Firemen in the Works were on-call about every other week and averaged about two call-outs in that week. William Harber became a part-time fireman in the 1930s and together with William Bown, they were the first aiders for the station. William of course lived in the GWR estate, so it was more or less a formality to get his son Bert onto the strength, and he joined in 1939. Bert said:

> There were several father and sons in our fire brigade. You got 6s and 6d a week for being on-call, which paid the rent, and there was the chance of more if you turned out of course. We went straight from work and did half-hour training four evenings a week and an hour, sometimes two, on Sunday mornings.

If a fire call went out, the chief was called first, but not all calls were for fires by any means. A list of the various tradesmen on-call was displayed in the fire station. If, for instance, a plumber was required because of a burst pipe or a crew was needed to take out a breakdown train, one of the firemen was sent off on a bicycle to knock them up. If a person was killed under

The Works fire brigade in 1950 with the Avon Cup and diploma. Left to right: Jimmy Little, Bert Harber, Ron Adams, Ray Sealy, Arthur O'Farrell, Jessie Collett and H. Cripps. (B. Harber)

a train locally, by accident or design, the brigade would have to retrieve the body. A motor ambulance, complete with trained staff, was also available to be turned out for a fire call if required. In the 1930s, the 'first call' fire vehicle was a 1915 Dennis Bros fire engine. In 1942 it was replaced by a modern Dennis engine. The earlier vehicle was retained for a while; its last major action was when the largest of the Works' gas holders was hit by enemy attack in 1942. This fine-looking vehicle is now preserved in the Steam Museum, still in the livery of the period. Two early horse-drawn steam pumps, probably built by Merryweather, were kept in the station, even though they had been obsolete for many years. They eventually went for scrap in wartime.

Alan Lambourn remembers seeing Mr Sealy, the fire officer, coming to work from his house in Church Place in the early 1950s. 'He always wore a very smart dark blue suit and was one of the few who still favoured a bowler at that time,' said Alan. Mr Sealy retired in about 1954 and Sid Smith took over. Sid also had a son Harold in the service. After nationalisation, if not before, all fire extinguishers for the Western were serviced in the Works' fire station workshop. The 50ft tower in the station yard was for hanging up the hoses after use; they were then rolled up dry and stored. The Works' brigade could, in theory, be called on to assist the borough brigade fight a fire in the town. The only problem there was that the two brigades used different couplings; the Works used screw fitting and the borough instantaneous fit. 'Some of the firemen in the late 1950s were Doug Mitcher, Alan Puffett, Ian Sawyer and full-timers Bill Grace and Eric Carter,' said Bert (see photograph above for more names).

INSPECTING AND TESTING MATERIALS

Samples of basic materials or ready-to-use commodities purchased by the Stores Department were checked and tested at various sites around the Works. The research laboratory, next to the fire station in Bristol Street, carried out a range of chemical, metallurgical and bacteriological work. Mr Dawe was the chief chemist for many years; he succeeded his boss Mr Davison in 1935. As already mentioned, samples from the Works' own brass, cast iron and non-ferrous furnaces were analysed here too. Some assistant chemists were employed just to analyse the water supplies. They visited water-softening plants from which the water for boilers was supplied. The chemists at Swindon also decided the rate charged by the company for carrying perishable goods, and it was they who would investigate if a claim was made regarding deterioration of such goods.

The materials and inspection section was attached to the Stores Department. Mr Phillips was the chief inspector here in the late 1930s and throughout the 1940s, with a staff of about twenty-seven. They carried out physical tests on random samples and visual checks which were done in the warehouses. Machines for testing tensile strength and elongation were used; others accelerated ageing or checked hardness. Steel, copper plates, wheels and timber were inspected before they left the contractor's works. Physical tests on materials were also carried out on the loco side in the 'test house'. This building was mainly concerned with the preparation, maintenance and testing of wrought iron, steel chain and hemp-rope lifting tackle. They also dealt with hand-operated chain pulley blocks.

THE GASWORKS

The company made their own gas at the extreme north of the Works' site, in the largest privately owned plant of its kind in the world. Power for the Works was provided by sixteen gas engines, coupled direct to electric generators working at 250 volts. It was said that the factory gasworks produced more gas than Gorse Hill Works, which supplied the rest of the town. It was rebuilt after the First World War using vertical retorts, whereby gas coal was descended through the red-hot retorts and converted to coke; the resultant vapours and gases rose and were drawn off. Each day the gasworks would carbonise 240 tons of coal, giving approximately three million cubic feet of gas. These figures were given in company publicity in 1924 and were the same as those given in 1950, so I would say they were very approximate. Bert Harber was an office boy here in 1937. Bert said:

> There were three clerks, a chief and two. I had to take paperwork to other offices and deliver messages to people who could not be contacted by phone, the usual duties of 'the boy'. I also wrote out coal tickets for the staff and assisted with the labelling of coal wagons returning to the collieries. Copying letters for the clerks was tricky; you had to place a damp tissue over them and put the two under a press.

Men in the gasworks were classed as either engine or boilerhouse workers, or gas or retort workers. They worked round the clock in three shifts. Throughout the works use was made of temporary labour available in the 1930s due to unemployment. Bert remembers the winter of 1937 when coal wagons couldn't deliver coal to the gasworks due to the severe weather. Thirty men arrived from the labour exchange to shovel coal from the stockpile.

A Mr Ackroyd was the manager in 1937 and Mr Jefferies was foreman with Mr Wilcox as chief clerk and Ernie Wordsell was the timekeeper. Leonard Lucas was a full-time painter here. Together with his mate, they painted lovely country scenes around the walls of the meter house. 'The workforce did not seem to mix with other railway workers or visit the rest of the works as I remember,' said Bert. The gasworks closed completely in early 1959.

8

THE OFFICES AND MANAGEMENT

The Chief Mechanical Engineer was the senior person in the department. He was responsible for all the mechanical and electrical work of the company. Workshop and office personnel based in the Works and depots, including Swindon, came under his control; so did running shed grades, enginemen and carriage and wagon maintenance staff and cleaners. The docks, too, were managed jointly by the chief docks manager, Cardiff, the chief (civil) engineer, Paddington and the Chief Mechanical Engineer, Swindon. The principle assistant to the CME was next in seniority. All senior staff had assistants who were normally expected to succeed them upon retirement. The company nearly always adopted the controversial system of promoting staff at all levels, by seniority and not by capability. Next in line was the running superintendent and outdoor assistant to the CME. He was usually chosen from the most senior and experienced of the divisional locomotive superintendents. Each division had a loco superintendent, an assistant and a mechanical inspector who would all have their offices at the principle running shed of their division. The CME's assistants, together with the chief draughtsman and chief clerk, and of course their assistants, were collectively known as the CME's 'personal staff'. The locomotive works' manager at Swindon was considered a weightier position than his counterpart on the carriage and wagon side. He had five assistants, to manage either factory or outstation work. Few in the CME management were promoted from senior supervisory positions.

Selbourne Smith's route to the top was fairly typical of those with exceptional ability. He distinguished himself as an apprentice on the loco side and went into the drawing office via the test house. After a number of senior locomotive positions at divisional level, he became assistant loco works manager at Swindon in 1948 and later got the top job at the age of forty-seven. The younger the man when he was promoted, the higher he would go. This was because of the policy on the GWR of strict internal selection of staff for more senior positions. A good example of this is the well-known story concerning the very popular and capable Mr Stanier. He accepted the top job on the LMS because he was only slightly younger than his boss Mr Collett, and would be too old to succeed him at Swindon when the time came. In 1930, Mr F.C. Hall was assistant running superintendent. He later moved up to locomotive running superintendent and outdoor assistant to the CME before becoming principle assistant to the CME in 1941. At that time, Mr K.J. Cook was works assistant, then principle assistant to the CME when Frederick Hall retired in 1947. In 1949, K.J.C. became head of department when Mr Hawksworth retired. Jack Dymond had become an eminent engineer in the Works by the 1940s and in 1957 made a very unconventional move from assistant to the mechanical engineer to take control of the stores, which by then had become the Supplies and Contracts Department.

After nationalisation, university graduates with technical engineering training took junior management positions in the department and some suitably qualified men now came in

Left: Mr Charles Crump OBE retired in 1931 from the senior post of Locomotive Running Superintendent and Outdoor Assistant to the Chief Mechanical Engineer at Swindon. (*GWR Magazine*)

Below: A young Henry Dening at the start of his career in a workshop office. (B. Carter)

An early office view. The sloping desks had nearly all been replaced throughout the offices by the 1940s. (BR National Railway Museum)

from outside firms or other railway companies. The training included working alongside gangs in the workshops, and prolonged periods away at college. The new British Railways administration, the Railway Executive, split up the CME Dept. The word 'Chief' in the title was dropped because the carriage and wagon section, as well as outdoor machinery, were no longer under the control of that person. Mr Cook was known as Mechanical and Electrical Engineer and his 'No.2' was Mr Pellow, the Motive Power Superintendent and Outdoor Assistant to the M&EE. Mr Creighton was made electrical assistant, which together with the motive power superintendent was a newly created post due to the reorganisation. Although the motive power depots were separate, the offices of the MP superintendent were within the Works. Mr Randle, who had been works assistant to the CME, became C&W engineer in 1950. This was a new position, alongside the C&W manager, Mr H.G. Johnson. Under the old GWR administration and until Mr Hawksworth retired, the C&W manager was under the control of the CME.

The Chief Accountants Department at Swindon was divided up into Costing, Departmental and New Work, Enginemen's and Firemen's Mutual Assurance Society, Final Accounts, Rolling Stock, Mechanical, Statistics, (Factory) Stores and Wages. This was the breakdown in 1952 and no doubt it had changed little since the amalgamation of the loco and carriage/wagon accounts in the 1930s. Most of the general accounts were centralised in the CME's block. This tall L-shaped building had evolved in earlier times with several major extensions and little effort was made to disguise the fact. A second floor had been added to the original part of the office block to accommodate a drawing office in 1904. It was, and still is, sited in the 'angle' between the mainline and the Gloucester branch. The drawing office was divided into three sections; the carriage and wagon section occupied the north wing, and the locomotive section the east wing. Part of the general drawing office was in the middle, together with an estimating office where costs could be calculated from the drawings. Another part of the general drawing office, together with the print room where drawings were copied, was on top of 'B' Shed and was reached by a walkway from the main office. The D.O. stores were a little distance away on the other side of 'B' Shed. The chief draughtsmen from the 1930s onward were Mr Smith, Mr Mattingly, and in the 1950s it was Mr Scholes. 'Ole Charlie Dunford was in charge of the drawing office clerks when I first started,' said George.

Over the three decades some offices inevitably moved, were renamed, amalgamated or occasionally became obsolete; information given here relates to the layout after 1945. The offices on the loco side had numbers but were better known by the type of work done. There were the estimating, engine records, motive power, correspondence, storehouse (accounts, administration and a separate personnel records), ledger, rolling stock, general, police, storage and distribution of fuel, mileage, personnel, and progress offices, as well as a stationery stores. The old loco works security office was on the ground floor of the CME building. A toilet block stood next to these offices, presumably built after the original inside toilets became the ladies' toilet. The Research and Development (R&D) office moved to a larger site above the new telephone exchange in the early 1950s.

The carriage and wagon (C&W) offices at Swindon formed the façade of the large fitting and machine ('No.15') shop just to the north-west of the station. This building was probably the most striking of any seen by the rail travellers. As you looked at it, some of the general stores were on the right, with the stores offices above. On the left were the managers' offices, the time office, the drawing office and the registrar's office. Above them were the progress office, accounts and chief clerks offices, and until 1952, the wages office. After the wages had moved, it became 'No.6', the cost office with George Ruddle in charge. The C&W block also had staff and records sections. There was a correspondence office, special loads office and a drawing stores. Mr Evans was carriage and wagon works manager in the 1930s. Mr Johnson took over this post in the 1940s. His assistant was Mr Colton, and C&W chief clerk from 1931–48 was Mr Ford. Later, under the Railway Executive, the office of the carriage and wagon engineer moved across to the east wing of the CME building on the first floor with the mechanical engineer.

Mr Kelynack was the chief accountant in the 1930s with Frank Bailey and Harold Gardner, his assistants. In 1941 Mr Gardner took over the department. The new chief was a member of the Town Council and had been Mayor of Swindon. He was also the last honorary treasurer of the GWR Medical Fund, taking over from his former boss Mr Kelynack in 1946. Along with others from the factory, Mr Gardner also lectured at the college some evenings. Here, there was an engineering department, as well as classes for business accounts and bookkeeping. Following nationalisation direct control of the CME and stores accounts and statistics were transferred to the chief accountant at Paddington, Mr Dashwood. Mr Gardner was then appointed assistant to accountant (rolling stock and stores) Western Region, but remained the most senior clerk at Swindon, (even after the war there were 600 clerks at Swindon, excluding the clerks who worked in the Stores Department) his No.2 was Cliff Sanders. Although he was fifty-five years of age in 1948, Mr Gardner worked on for about ten more years.

The retirement's section in the staff magazines showed many of the accounts people in the department during the period left with forty-five years of service; a few managed nearly fifty years, as they were allowed to work beyond the age of sixty. Because works and office staff could be retained during the war, some 'clocked up' more than that. A Mr J. Street managed fifty-seven years by the time he was released in 1946, nearly all in the East time office. There was no age limit at which senior officers had to retire and this applied to departmental heads as well, although they would not be able to hang on to office as long as their bosses in the 1930s, Mr Collett and Mr Auld. Mr Collett, the CME, reluctantly retired at the age of seventy, not because of pressure he got from the board, but because his principal assistant Mr Auld, also seventy, would not stay on any longer and support his cause.

The whole of the CME Dept accounts was based at Swindon Works and it was said that only about one in three clerks at Swindon dealt with factory work. The three largest accounts offices were '21', '22' and '26'. They would have up to fifty clerks working in each at any one time. The 'clerk in charge' of these larger offices was senior in status to his equivalent in one of the smaller offices and graded a special 'C'. Some offices had a raised area at one end where the clerk in charge and his assistant had their desks. Anyone of lower rank who needed to speak to the person in charge did so by respectfully standing at the bottom of the steps. This had the effect, intentional or not, of making them feel even more intimidated than ever. The offices in the CME's block were centrally heated and had large iron radiators. They had high ceilings and large windows, so they were light but poorly ventilated. Each window frame held two sets of sash windows, one behind the other, to minimise noise and fumes from the nearby workshops. The majority of men smoked a pipe or cigarettes. Unlike the workshops, there had been no smoking ban prior to 1939, so if the windows were closed it was stuffy and if they were open it was noisy. Barbara Carter said:

> A lot of women in the offices smoked as well. I didn't because my father suffered badly with asthma and I thought I might get it if I smoked. The double sets of windows were very effective at keeping out the noise and of course the fumes of the shops nearby, as long as you did not open them. One of the girls in my office made herself unpopular by keep wanting to open them.

Each section had a telephone and outside lines were available via the exchange. By the 1950s every double desk had a phone and some people were able to dial straight out to the General Post Office (GPO) network. Clocks were made by smiths and were connected to an electrical circuit driven by a master clock in 'No. 8' office. Mechanical clocks were checked and wound by a fellow known as 'clocky'. He would go round the Works on a bike and also did any repairs, cleaning and adjustments. All offices kept selections of reference books and books of conversion tables. Personnel could obtain 'rough books' from the stores, which were hardcover books impressed with the company initials. The blotter doubled as a directory of names and extension numbers for when help was needed with a problem. A good clerk soon worked out who to ask for and who to avoid when contacting other departments. Within either the loco or carriage sides, office people all seemed to know one another, at least by name. They had more opportunity to integrate at work than the shop workers. Some bad feelings towards clerks who remained loyal to the company during the general strike of 1926 persisted through the 1930s but generally fizzled out after 1939. There was no need of a night shift in the offices, shop clerks excepted, and in any case the company knew that the efficiency of the clerk was significantly reduced at night due to progressive fatigue.

Academics undertook further education in accounting. Several evenings a week at night school, they attended the Swindon and North Wilts Technical School, which, by the 1930s, was better known as 'the College'. Up until the 1930s, the brightest students had been able to go on to study at the London School of Economics (LSE). Here they would attend the railwayman's department one evening a week after work, with a day spent there for the annual examination. Senior clerks at Swindon, Messrs Dening, Minchin, Gardner and Sanders, among others, gained the Brunel medal earlier in their careers for consistently high marks each year during their studies at the LSE. From 1929 the Churchward Testamonial Fund awarded a number of book prizes each year to the best students in the department, to encourage education in engineering and commerce. The trustees of the fund, Messrs Hawksworth, Auld and Kelynack, considered the results obtained throughout the year. Most of the awards came to Swindon because they provided much of the CME Dept training. The money came from a fund set up at the suggestion and initial contribution of Mr Churchward himself when he retired in 1921.

Barbara Carter's family, like most in Swindon, had several members that spent all their working lives in the railway. Her grandfather Richard retired in 1931 as president of the Foremen's Association and chief foreman of the carriage fitters in '3', '15', '15A', '18' and '19D' shops. Her father Henry (known at work as Harry) became clerk in charge of '22' office and

Ladies from the loco side typist section attending the wedding of one of their colleagues at Christchurch in 1930. Sixth from the left is section head Freda Dening. (B. Carter)

The stores accounts office on the second floor of the CME block in the 1940s. Irene Dening is the only one identified (third row on the left). (B. Carter)

Barbara's two aunts, Freda and Irene, achieved high honour 'inside'; they started in the Works accounts in 1913 and 1915. 'They may have gone in as shorthand typists,' said Barbara. At that time, there were few females on that sort of work 'inside' or anywhere else on the GWR. Like their older brother, Freda and Irene had also won the Brunel medal for shorthand and advanced bookkeeping respectively. 'These were the only such awards to go to females as far as I know,' said Barbara, and the only time when three were awarded in one family, in 1920, 1921 and 1922. Freda retired a bit early in about 1960. She was, by then, in charge of the loco side's typists. Irene Dening held an unknown senior position in stores accounts from at least 1932. She worked her full term and was personal assistant to the stores superintendent when she retired.

Barbara Carter started in 'No.40' office in 1940. This office was nicknamed 'White City' for some unknown reason. With a favourable report from her school, The Elms at Faringdon, Barbara said that 'this was enough for the company to consider me at that time'. In common with most school leavers, Barbara took the school's certificate examination before the end of her final term. She decided to continue her studies at the College after work to advance her career; this was her choice, as the company did not insist on it. She said:

> We worked twelve-hour shifts but I left work early on night school evenings so as to be there from 6 p.m. to 9 p.m. It was a long day, having been in the blacked-out factory since 8 a.m. I also managed to get away early on Thursdays to attend the Wesleyan Guild, my weekly social evening out.

For the first six months she was using an advanced Muldivo machine, calculating timber measurement and prices. 'There were eight ladies to a section here, including the section head. My first net wage in 1940 was 5s 8d. I still have that first (very austere) payslip.'

Barbara's friends and colleagues included Marjorie Parsons, whose mother conducted the Swindon Ladies Choir, and Doreen Pullen. Doreen was an impersonator in her spare time; she travelled round locally with a party entertaining the troops. Ivy Davis ran a sort of magazine club in the office. Barbara said that 'each of us bought a different woman's magazine, which, after we had read it, was passed on to Ivy who redistributed them among the contributors'. Another co-operative scheme enabled Barbara and some of her colleagues to buy savings certificates which the government was promoting during the war. Barbara said that 'twenty of us got together and all paid in a shilling a week. A certificate was purchased and every twenty weeks each person received one'. Reg Cook used to come and have his tea in our office. He was in charge of the storehouse where all the old documents were kept. Barbara said that 'he always looked scruffy probably because the old papers got very dusty. To supplement his low pay, Reg would get you scarce items on the black market'. George remembers Reg only had one eye, 'possibly due to an injury in the Great War'.

'White City' was on the first floor of the CME's building, above the cash office and the 'money makeup' section. Part of it was the accounts machine room. Across the corridor was the stores machine room. Some older staff still called it by its former name, the addressograph office, although that type of machine was now only one of a range of different types used there. Glass screens separated the desks from the machines. Around the walls of the office were fitted cabinets containing the punchcards and, in common with all offices, cupboards of stationery and ledgers. Percy Richards was in overall charge of the machine sections and Muriel Whale was section chief over the sorter and tabulator machine operators: 'Mr Richards rode an upright bicycle down from Old Town every day to work (something I tried for a while). Some evenings and weekends he served as a major in the Home Guard. Because I was the quickest typist in the office, he would get me to do all the Home Guard paperwork.'

After being there a few years, Barbara was required to go and issue coal tickets to retired workmen on alternate Tuesday afternoons. This was done from an office in the former mess rooms near the 'tunnel entrance'. This job appears to have been given to anyone that could be spared, as Enid Hogden in the cash office also remembers going there on occasions. Later, Barbara was moved to the stores accounts, which was entirely separate from the CME accounts. Miss Foulds was in charge of their machine room and Barbara was the senior operator over the twelve to fifteen females on key-punching machines. These girls typed the information from cost statements into the machine, which then converted it and stamped it into punchcards as combinations of holes. Because of the strict divide between the two departments, there was some resentment at the appointment of the new section head.

Barbara's father, Henry, started his working life in a workshop office probably on the loco side in about 1906 or 1907. By the time he was twenty, he had gained his advanced bookkeeping qualifications, which took him three years. Later, Barbara told him jokingly that she would beat that, which she did, but then admits the course time was condensed due to wartime conditions. Mr Dening senior also taught at night school to help make ends meet, but he must have progressed quickly. Barbara remembers him telling her his salary had reached £400 per annum; this is thought to have been in the early 1930s when a Grade 1 clerk with five years experience received no more than £350. Mr Dening, a Methodist, gives us some idea of the conduct observed in the office in the late 1930s and early '40s, when he told his daughter he only had to look up from his desk and any talking stopped. She remembers the story because he went on to say 'wearing my spectacles for short sightedness, I couldn't actually see a thing when I looked up but nobody ever worked that out'. Just after the war, Mr Dening suddenly lost his voice and could only faintly whisper. Because of this, he was given a single office, still on the first floor next to those of the chief clerk and his assistant. He communicated by writing notes, to which sometimes the reply would be written down as well, something he found very amusing. Harry Dening died while at work in 1947, and after a period under the deputy, Mr Minchin, Frank Dance took over as clerk in charge of '22' office. It was during his time as 'acting clerk in charge' that Mr Minchin had to ask Barbara Carter (*née* Dening) if he could borrow her late father's notebooks so he could properly manage the office. 'He obviously felt uncomfortable about asking,' said Barbara.

Each office had an office junior. They were the most recently appointed employees, usually a girl or boy just out of school before becoming a junior clerk at eighteen years of age. Achieving this was still dependant on a 'good conduct' report and passing the examination. There were plenty of jobs available outside at that time. Yvonne Hodey (*née* Jones) said: 'I could have gone into the departmental stores, Morse's or McIlroy's, or factories such as Wills's and Compton's.' But she passed her medical in January 1953 and started work 'inside' the following month. Yvonne was an office junior with a single desk at the back of '21 Accounts CME'. She said:

> The office was vast, about forty or fifty staff, both men and women. It was very daunting at first. I was positioned in a 'cubby hole' out of sight but within earshot of the clerk in charge and his assistant. I remember Mr Rendall and Mr Nash, who were in charge in '21' office at the time.

Yvonne made the tea, ran messages and collected or delivered post to Mr Chesterman in the correspondence office. She said that 'this was in the days when you called your elders "Mr" or "Miss" … and never by their Christian name, unless invited to do so'. She was also trusted to take money to the bank regularly, sometimes quite large sums, for Mr Roberts, who was the clerk in charge of the central wages office, and Mr Sanders, the assistant chief accountant. Yvonne said:

> I took the money in a large canvas cash bag. One time a policeman stopped me and told me I should not be out walking with all that money; this was money paid in for concessionary bus and rail tickets, which was either taken at the cash office or arrived there from the works booking office to be bagged up on its way to the bank. Making the tea was fun. This was a

major operation, as it was done in very little space under the large staircase with about six other girls from different offices. Carrying large trays of tea for the whole office up and down the stairs was tricky to say the least. Then we had to wash up and do a repeat performance in the afternoon.

The staff, Yvonne remembered, in '21' office included Mr West, Mr Harris, Mr Youll and Don Curtis, as well as Miss Wykeham-Martin, Winnie Stroud and Dorothy Wirdham. Yvonne said:

> At that time Jennifer Allen was 'the Junior' in '22' office. Cecilia Brown and Janet Knighton were office girls I knew who worked elsewhere in the department. Most people had close relatives working there. All I had was my cousin Maureen Stokes who was in the manager's office since grandfather Stevenson had retired before the war.

After nine months, Yvonne became a junior clerk and was moved to what she remembers as the Powers-Samas Department (another section of the accounts machine room, of which 'Pop' Richards was still the chief in 1953). This was just down the corridor from '21' office on the first floor of the CME building. Here she operated punchcard machines. Her net pay then started at 25s.

George Petfield left school and started his working life in the offices of the CME Dept in 1944. He was interviewed by 'Don' Rendall. George recalled:

> I later found out that Mr Rendall was clerk in charge of 'No.1' office and the third most senior clerk in the department [Later, in the 1960s, Mr Rendall got the top job of works accountant]. It was all very informal. When I asked when I should start, I was told 'start tomorrow'.

Mr Rendall started George on 'departmental accounts', calculating costs of work being done for or by other departments – in his case, the costs of outstation work. George's bosses in his office, '22 Accounts CME' were Henry (Harry) Dening and his assistant Tom Minchin. Tom was a Methodist preacher in his spare time. He was also an accomplished orator, and along with his boss, Mr Gardner, had won awards for public speaking at the GWR Music Festival.

George's salary was £98 per year when he started in 1944, leaving him below the figure at which he would start paying tax, and this included an hour's compulsory overtime per day under special wartime arrangements. The offices started work at 8 a.m. instead of the pre-war 9 a.m. After the war, the start time changed permanently to 8.30 a.m. George still had to be on the 7.25 a.m. train from Wootton Bassett; only now he could have a look for any new locomotives that had arrived in the reception sidings overnight. A bell sounded in the offices at the start and finish of the shifts. George remembered:

> Dinnertime was 12.23 p.m. to 1.35 p.m. That never altered. After 1954, I remember the roar of the up 'Bristolian', which would remind us to get things up together before going home. The afternoon shift finished at 5.22 p.m. It was then a mad dash out through the tunnel and along to the station to be on the 'all stations to Temple Meads via Badmington' in exactly ten minutes.

On Friday, overtime started at 5.45 p.m. Duties then included meeting at the cash office at 8.30 a.m. and proceeding to a pay point to pay night workers at 9.00 p.m. Overtime in the CME's accounts was worked more towards the end of the financial year, when the books were brought up to date for inspection by the auditors. If necessary, office staff were expected to stay behind to catch up, although they were rarely there more than half an hour a day, as overtime payment then became claimable. The accounts were scrutinised by auditors based at Swindon and annually by public auditors appointed by the shareholders.

After six months of employment, George was entitled to concessionary or privileged rail travel. This was a generous 25 per cent of standard fare. When he went off to do his national service in July 1945, George lost this for the forces rate of 66 per cent. 'I remember that 7s and 11d got you a Swindon to Paddington standard return at the privileged rate in the late 1940s, and for several years to follow,' he said. After his national service in the Royal Air Force (RAF) working on pay accounts, George returned to the Works and his chair was about 4ft from the one he had vacated two and a half years earlier. He was now working on personal accounts. His section handled claims against outside firms and individuals for damage or fraud. Back in 1944–45 a lot of his colleagues had been men who should have retired on reaching sixty, if it was not for the war. So when he returned in 1948, the office seemed to be full of newcomers. Men and women clerks returning from the war might talk about the lighter side of their experiences but others never mentioned it at all. There was a lot of anti-German feeling at the time. Clerk Harold Tanner was asked what he was studying at night school when interviewed for promotion. He said, 'German, so as to make new friends.' The answer ensured he remained in his present position.

A few familiar faces from 1944–45 were still there or dispersed throughout the department, such as Frank Davis, Cliff Sanders, Syd Carnsew, John Partridge, Guy Hemmings, Grace Clack and Isaac Carter, formerly works' cashier. Inevitably, romances were formed in such a close-knit group. Pam Sheppard was there at that time and later married David Coombs from loco wages. 'I don't remember seeing Winnie Chowles, the most senior woman in accounts when I returned. She may have retired in the meantime,' said George. Charlie Selman was still in '22' office. He dealt with cost accounts for docks and waterways. Often spending time away in South Wales, he retired about 1950. His brother George was a section chief in '21' office and had served as Mayor. Quite a number in the offices had come up from the absorbed railway companies of South Wales and general alterations were carried out to accommodate them. George Eynon came from the Barry Railway and was in the local GW Savings Bank for a while. Frank Davies had been on the Brecon and Merthyr. Others had been transferred to outstations, which in this case meant offices elsewhere on the system. Mr Gardner, the chief accountant or 'office assistant to the CME' to give him his proper title, came into the Works as early as 1907, and Archie Jefferies, George's first section chief, had started in 1912. But most of the senior staff at the time had joined the company in the following ten years.

George travelled in to work from Wootton Bassett on the 07.25 a.m. one morning when the train suddenly came to a stop in the cutting. Looking out of the window they could see a bull walking down the track towards them. The animal ambled past the train, allowing them to proceed without too much delay. But the 28XX with coal empties for South Wales had to follow the bull all the way to Bassett, at walking pace. This is one of several stories told by old Swindon people about cattle or horses holding up workmen's trains.

Most Swindon girls leaving school did not want to work in any of the local factories if they could avoid it. Even factory offices were frowned upon by them, and their mothers! The railway works, however, was different and a position in the CME's offices was *the* place of choice. The brightest girls from Headlands and Commonweal grammar schools went 'inside' and some school leavers went on to study bookkeeping at the College's commercial department while waiting to go in. Having a father in accounts helped but there was still the entrance test and medical before acceptance. All medical examinations for CME staff were done at Park House which was on the corner of the GWR estate. By the late 1930s, representations were being made on behalf of female staff as to the setting up of a pension scheme. Many of those who had joined during the First World War were approaching that time in their lives when they realised that having such a scheme would be advantageous. The directors agreed to this in 1938, for female clerks. At this time the company as a whole employed 1,831 female clerks.

Ladies monopolised the typists' office and machine rooms on the first floor. Here, their prospects for promotion, especially in the machine room, were better than anywhere else in accounts. The company acknowledged that female operators were faster and better when using

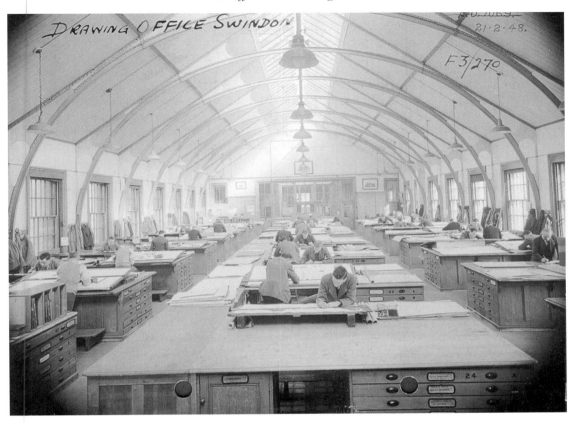

This view shows the larger loco, carriage and wagon section of the Drawing Office in 1948. (Author's collection)

accounting machinery than men. Women and girls first came into the Works in any numbers during the First World War and this valuable source of labour was continued thereafter. Upon getting married, females were required to resign, although this did not apply in wartime and presumably from 1945 onwards, as when Barbara Dening left to be married – becoming Barbara Carter – in 1950. It was her husband, not her employer, who expected his wife to stay at home. When it was known that a person in the office or shop was to be married, it was usual to have a collection and presentation of a gift to wish them well. Barbara said:

> When the person leaving arrived in the morning, they found colleagues had come in early and decorated their desk. A poem and some words offering marital advice would be prominent amongst the embellishment. They were allowed to leave a few minutes early in the evening to a cacophony of banging noises, and as they passed the other offices they heard the din and joined in.

9

OUTDOOR AND FACTORY MAINTENANCE

The work of maintaining a fleet of 3,600 locomotives, nearly 9,000 carriages and over 80,000 wagons by the company's CME Dept is well known and well documented, and even the other departments within the company called it simply 'The Locomotive Dept'. However, there was a huge amount of other mechanical equipment around the system that Swindon or the other CME depots were responsible for, and little is recorded of this. Some men spent part of their time away from the workshops and offices; some spent all their working lives away. The 'D' shop (carpenters and bricklayers) checkboard, for one, continuously displayed outstation checks for some who were officially based there.

Mechanical equipment at depots, docks and at the lineside, such as cranes, hoists, turntables, water tanks and columns, water-softening plants and moveable bridges, were usually built by outside firms but installed by the CME Dept. They were responsible for the moving parts of this outdoor mechanical equipment and any water supplies. All replacement parts were drawn from 'E' warehouse in the carriage and wagon stores. Of the five assistants of the (locomotive) works' manager, three were for outstation and outdoor machinery. There was also an outdoor machinery assistant to the CME. Gangs of men, based mainly in the 'L2' tank and 'PL' platelayers' shops, would go out to maintain the water troughs, and with them would go the tool and mess vans. The galvanised steel plate troughs were 6in deep, 18in wide and up to 1,838ft long. They were bolted between the 'four foot' at strategic points along the mainlines. With full-line occupation and temporary speed restrictions in the opposite direction, the 10ft sections of troughs were removed, repaired and replaced. The permanent way gangs also took the opportunity to work on the track, thus minimising the interference to the flow of traffic. The job was done mainly during the night and could take any time up to a week before the up and down mainline troughs could be refilled with water. Meanwhile, locomotives on non-stop trains would have to make an unscheduled stop at a station to fill up at the water column.

The Severn Tunnel ran through severely waterlogged land and millions of tons of water were allowed to drain into the tunnel daily. This stopped pressure building up but then that water had to be raised. Pumping stations were situated on both sides of the estuary, two at Sudbrook on the Welsh side and another known as 'sea wall' on the English side. Electrical and mechanical gangs from Swindon usually stayed outstation there for weeks at a time to do the maintenance and repairs of the boiler houses, the old Cornish beam engines and pumps, with most of the work being done onsite. A lot of time was spent underground replacing or repairing the suction and delivery valves and bucket plungers. From the late 1950s, the Cornish engines were being replaced by electrified pumps and Swindon provided the manpower.

Men went out daily to the electric and steam pumps at the pumping station just north of Kemble railway station. Kemble was found to be the nearest supply of water containing the

The boiler house at Seawall pumping station on the Gloucester side of the Severn tunnel. (*GWR Magazine*)

The boiler house at '5 Miles, 4 Chains' pumping station on the Welsh side of the Severn tunnel. (*GWR Magazine*)

The cylinder floor at Sudbrooke pumping station showing parts of the Cornish beam engines. (*GWR Magazine*)

reduced levels of chemical salts required to minimise the 'fur up' of boilers. For the efficient use of steam boilers, it was essential that the water supply was 'clean and soft', which meant free from impurities and chemicals, particularly lime. A thirteen-mile pipeline brought the water from Kemble to the works at Swindon. The pipes and any landslips due to leakage was also the responsibility of the CME Dept. Swindon shed sent a pannier tank loco to Kemble once a month, so that steam could be supplied to the earlier pumps while their boilers were shut off for maintenance.

All boiler inspectors were attached to the CME Dept and all boiler tests were carried out by them. They also went out periodically and examined the air receivers and safety valves of petrol-driven machines in their division and they would arrange for any repairs to be done by their department. All the company's stationary steam boilers were worked and maintained by the staff of the CME Dept; the only exception was its marine boilers. The stationary Cornish, Lancashire, Yorkshire, vertical crane and stationary locomotive boilers were repaired by locomotive fitters, as were steam road rollers. Road rollers belonged to the engineering department but the CME Dept tested and issued their drivers with certificates. The larger stationary boilers could consume more than a ton of coal per day but the men who looked after them, apart from 'firing them competently and economically', were required to service them and report immediately any defects in operation. When cold, the boiler had to be washed out. This was done ideally once a week, preferably on a Saturday, together with the cleaning of the firebox and tubes. Mountings, such as safety valves, clack valves, and feed pumps had to be kept free of deposits. Blow-off cocks, test cocks and water-gauge passages had to be regularly cleaned and greased. Periodic examinations were carried out by the boiler inspector or responsible boilersmith, depending on type and boiler pressure. A Mr Jefferies was chief boiler inspector in the CME Dept in the 1940s. Records of boiler examinations and hydraulic tests were kept and checked regularly by the foreman or inspector. The person responsible for the steam machinery was known as the 'driver'. He was expected to keep the bearings and brasses sufficiently lubricated without being wasteful, to avoid increased wear and overheated bearings. He had to make adjustments to oscillating parts and bearings when necessary, so as to prevent knocking. And he could perform minor repairs or stop the machinery immediately if any problems arose. If the machinery was to be stopped for any length of time, he would grease frictional surfaces against corrosion.

During the war, electricians from 'E' shop worked outstation on new cranes being built at various South Wales docks. Two or three men, and sometimes apprentice Bert Harber, worked 6 a.m. to 8 p.m. under licence to Stothard and Pitt. They came home every other Saturday morning until Monday morning. The other weekend they came back just overnight for a bath and change of clothes. Men worked outstation, removing the steam heating hoses from carriage stock during the summer. The hoses were sent to Swindon for testing and repair or replacement by the 'steam gang'. These men dealt with all the steam heating apparatus used on rolling stock. Hydraulic capstans used in shunting yards regularly required new trunion valves. Some staff based in the drawing office regularly went out to depots to evaluate complaints about locomotives and rolling stock. These people were the 'experimental gang' and would, when requested by the Running Department, travel on the footplate or in the train to investigate, and if necessary redesign the offending parts. Fitters from 'A' shop went out on the footplate of locomotives, recently overhauled or 'ex-works', to make any adjustments while the engine was in steam. Usually the same men who had reassembled what should have been the steam-tight pipework went out. They knew which threads were left or right handed.

Unlike the 'experimental gang', who investigated specific problems, technical assistants from the Research and Development section studied the general performance limitations of locomotives and rolling stock, with a view to improving them. In the 1950s, Sam Ell was the engineer in charge and Herbert Titchener (Titch) was his assistant. Mr Ell had been in the 'experimental section' of the drawing office most of his working life and by the late 1940s he was the senior person. When the new R&D section was formed and moved out in about 1950, he went with them. The late Ken Ellis, said of his former boss, 'his office [in 1956] was the most cluttered and untidy place I ever saw'.

Technical Assistants (TA) then were Ken Ellis, Mike Casey, Martin Lloyd, Ron Lucas, John Smith and Doug Stagg, amongst others. Ernie Nutty was the senior TA. Their work included measuring the performance of locomotives on the stationary test plant in 'A' shop and going out recording data under controlled conditions using the dynamometer car. This 48ft vehicle was equipped with scientific instruments for measuring the drawbar horsepower of the locomotive and wind resistance. Mr Ell and his team are best remembered for redesigning the draughting of express locomotives so effectively. TAs also went out with the whitewash car; a coach attached to the rear of the train which spilt white liquid onto the track when travelling over rough sections and was used as an indicator for the permanent way staff. Train timings and motive power requirements were worked out by this section, according to gradients and loads.

As well as financial allowances, the company conceded that an employee could not be doing the job he was employed to do all of his working time. In the CME Dept this mainly applied to men working outstation from Swindon or other depots where they were based. If he had to travel, including walking, to get to his place of work from where he booked on, an allowance was made for this. He was also paid a meal allowance if he was away from the 'home station' during his booked mealtime. The men negotiated, through their sectional council, an issue of protective clothing. In the rules and regulations, it stated that 'Any pay due to any employee leaving the service will not be paid until the uniform and all articles the property of the company, supplied to him, shall have been delivered up or satisfactorily accounted for'. In the 1930s and thereafter the working roster had to allow a minimum of twelve hours between shifts for a person working from their home station, and in all other cases nine hours minimum.

I have met several Swindon railwaymen who were fascinated by steam cranes, just as others are by steam locomotives. Swindon looked after the maintenance and repair of travelling cranes, following which they were load tested using flatbed wagons filled with cast-iron weights and fitted with lifting slings. There were always various types of cranes to be seen

Technical assistants Ron Lucas (left) and Martin Lloyd, some time in the late 1950s. The photographer thought the man in the background, doing the work of three men, was probably Ernie Nutty. (Ken Ellis/Author's collection)

around the Works and shed yards. Cranes awaiting works' attention were held on sidings that curved around the east side of the CME offices parallel with the Gloucester line. These sidings had pits, so that work could be carried there, as well as in 'G' shop, which had their crane repair area in 'B' shed. In the 1950s they were the responsibility of chargeman Ralph Angold. The locomotive department's crane drivers carried out their own routine maintenance on the steam and hand travelling cranes when they were back at their home depots. Swindon had about three 6-ton and one 12-ton travelling crane for use around the Works. They also had two large travelling cranes which were kept in 'G' shop yard. Work done by cranes around the Swindon factory included loading and unloading timber in the concentration yard, and lifting assembled trackwork in 'X' shop. If a 4.6.0. locomotive had overrun the turntable and the bogie had dropped over the pit, it was one of the big cranes that lifted the front end so it could be driven slowly back. A lot of the time cranes were standing idle during the week but were sent out in goods, and breakdown trains at weekends to do engineering work. George remembers chargeman Harold Couling from the early 1950s. He said: 'He could drive anything.' Harold was the 'G' shop chargeman responsible for allocating the labourers to their work routine. Other drivers remembered in the 1940s and '50s were Jack Norris, Claude Prince, Bill Ireson, Eddie Jones, Bob Waite, Norman Smith, Sam Jones, Dick Selwood and Les Smart, who later went into 'A' shop and drove a 100-ton crane.

Cranes on their own wheels, lifting loads, could be dangerous, especially without the careful use of the outriggers to stabilise them. Dick Selwood had to jump clear of his crane when the ground gave way while working on the new 'X' shop in the mid-1950s. During working hours, the outdoor assistant to the mechanical and electrical engineer, Joe Clarke, would often see the breakdown train away. He would always say 'no more than 10 per cent overload mind',

Crane men. Left to right: –?–, Vic, Corbett, –?–, Sam Jones, Fred Archer and Jack Bates. The 'Triangle', Swindon, on 22 July 1962. (R. Grainger)

which meant, be mindful that with the jib lowered the lifting capacity is much reduced. But often there was no choice, said John Brettell. The large cranes were often lifting more than they should because of the need to lower the jib to reach an adjacent load. The dangers of crane work were perhaps offset by the opportunity to earn good money through overtime, as crews could expect to be away for long periods. On the rare occasions that George Petfield was questioned by his boss as to why a man was receiving so much more than his normal wages, it was usually due to a timesheet submitted by a crane driver or his mate.

Steam cranes, together with their match trucks, formed part of the breakdown train; the rest of which was made up with mess/sleeping and tool vans, as well as a guard's van. The larger sheds in each division had a big 45-ton crane and a 36-tonner to go out with the breakdown train, sometimes two of each size. For many years the 'big-uns' at Swindon were 'No.2' and 'No.19', which were of 36- and 45-ton capacity respectively, built by Ransome and Rapier of Ipswich. The 45-ton crane was one of several ordered by the Railway Executive in the early part of the war. During the passage of a Royal Train, the depots along its route kept a crane in steam, together with breakdown vans and gangs, as well as standby locomotives. Crews liked the 'deepdene specials', as they were known, because they got overtime for doing next to nothing. The Swindon breakdown cranes were based in the Works, not in the running shed as was usual. The crew would be made up of the supervisor, who was a 'G' shop foreman, the crane driver and four or five groundsmen. The groundsmen were general assistants who went out with the cranes. They were paid a little more than labourers' rate. During the week, if not required to work outstation, these men worked as 'G' shop fitters' mates.

A full crew went out with the breakdown train, even for routine work, in case they were called away to a derailment. All work carried out on the permanent way, including the

The 50ft bed lathe in 'G' shop . The work set up is a 20ft-long dock gate cylinder. (BR National Railway Museum)

installation of bridge girders and viaduct maintenance, came under the control of the Civil Engineer's Department. Although other departments had their own cranes and crews, it was the CME Dept which passed all crane drivers as qualified to operate them. If a large load, such as bridge girders, were to be lifted, the two big cranes would go out in tandem. Most of this work was also done at weekends. As the big cranes overhung the adjacent tracks when swung round, they needed the occupancy of adjacent lines. A breakdown train, usually with the '36T' crane, regularly left Swindon at 2.00 a.m. to work at the engineering depot at Taunton, arriving back around teatime. During the war, the cross-Channel guns that were aimed at the Germans in occupied France had to have the 16in barrels replaced. Swindon's big cranes were sent down to Dover to help remove and replace the barrels, which were then brought back to the Works for relining.

Maintenance staff worked all round the factory site, as well as outstation, and could be on-call seven days a week. 'G' shop was the mechanical maintenance workshop. As well as crane parts and pumps, they maintained and repaired all the overhead lifting appliances in the Works. The eight Stirling boilers that generated steam for engines, steam hammers and heating was the responsibility of 'G' shop maintenance, as was the plant necessary for the central supply and distribution of electric, hydraulic and pneumatic power, as well as oxygen and acetylene for the shops that required it. All the heavy machinery 'inside' the Works was cared for by 'G' shop men, as was outstation equipment that could not be repaired on site. Hydraulic cylinders were bored on 'kearns' or the larger 'shanks' boring mills. Rams were machined on the Tangye lathe. This machine had capacity to take work up to 50ft long, such as the hydraulic rams that opened and closed dock gates. When it was installed, an internal wall had to be knocked through. Capstan rams were also repaired in this shop by mounting in a vertical boring mill. 'G' shop-based staff had a cabin in the rolling mills from where the bricklayers regularly had to replace the firebricks in the furnaces. This was just some of the many and varied types of work of the mechanical maintenance shop.

John Brettell moved from 'A' shop to 'G' shop in 1949. This workshop was still known as the old 'Millwrights' shop by some of the older men. Bill Brown was the head foreman in those days. He had taken over from a Mr Marshman in the 1930s. Mr Simpkins took over from Mr Brown, then in the late 1950s Harry Philpott became the 'G' shop foreman. It was not unknown for Mr Philpott to turn up in the workshop in the middle of the night if he was preoccupied with some work-related matter. John's first job was as a fitter in 'G' shop, then an outstation fitter. Later, he became a 'crane tester'. John said, 'Les Humphries and

Retirement presentation for Fred Selby, maintenance chargeman 'G' shop in 1953/54. In the front (left to right) are John Brettell, Foremen Bert Price and Harry Philpott, Bill Simpkins (chief foreman), Fred Selby and Charlie People (chargemen painters). Of the senior 'G'-shop staff at that time, only Jack Tyler (inspector) is missing. (J. Brettell)

I would go all over the Western Region to supervise the regular loading tests that had to be carried out'. His next move was to Grade 2 workshop inspector before becoming assistant engineer (cranes) in the drawing office. All the electrical, boiler and crane inspectors now came under him, a combined total of ten or twelve at Swindon and others throughout the Western Region. He in turn was answerable to the Assistant Mechanical and Electrical Engineer for Outdoor Machinery. John recalled:

> Each division would send in a report when they required work to be done. I would meet the engineers involved and submit a report to M&EE, detailing the conclusions reached. I would have to suggest how best to apply the department's cranes and resources and which depots would take on the work. The chief never once rejected my proposals.

'E' shop was the electrical maintenance and installations workshop for the factory and outstation. Like 'G' shop, they too had sections in other shops. Any work that could not be done on site was taken to 'E' shop. Electricians dealt with such things as machine tool motors, automatic train control (ATC) gear, lighting circuits, electric pumping stations, substations, cranes, and later permanent way machinery. Carriage lighting was the only electrical work they did not undertake; that was done in '5' shop. Bert Harber became an apprentice in 'E' shop in 1938 and was called up immediately upon completing his five years. 'There was no set programme of training. I just gained experience with each gang as determined by the foreman,' he said. Bert made a complete list of all the electrical personnel in 1938, which he

A 300-ton press which delivered hydraulic power in the form of high-pressure water to machinery around the Works. (*GWR Magazine*)

still has. Bert said that 'there were sixty men on the shop strength. The two foremen were Mr Sutcliffe and Mr Hugo. There were seven gangs, including my first with chargeman George Dan, and there were seven apprentices'. In 1942 they moved from their main base in a corner of 'O' shop to take over a part of 'D' shop. When Bert returned in 1947, the foremen who had stayed on past retirement had been replaced by Mr Money and Mr Hewitt.

The electricians had an ongoing programme of servicing machinery with the fitters, including working while the rest of the factory stopped for the annual holiday. For four years running in the 1950s, one of the 100-ton cranes in 'A' shop was overhauled. Bert remembers the work started at 5.20 p.m. on Friday as the day shift left. He said, 'We stripped all the electrical gear from the crane, as well as the motors and control gear, then refurbished it. The day before the end of the holiday, everything had to be back together ready for the testers to move in and do the load tests'.

Permanent way work had become more mechanised in the 1950s and a corner of 'B' shed, nicknamed 'the cage', became the track maintenance section for the Western Region. Ballast cleaners, tamping machines, track-laying machines and excavators were repaired here, as well as on site.

10

NATIONAL EMERGENCY AND NATIONALISATION

Those called up for war service were drawn from shop and office in roughly equal numbers. Some men felt a strong moral dilemma between doing their duty and potentially having to kill someone. For others, taking part clashed with their religious beliefs, but George Petfield remembers some of those very reluctant types actually went off and conducted themselves very well. Pacifists were amongst Swindon clerks sent to do work for the Ministry of Munitions at the relocated GWR Audit section at Aldermarston and again George heard they worked very well. The first to be conscripted were men up to the age of twenty-five – those whose work could theoretically be absorbed by the remaining workforce. They included apprentices, labourers, clerks, vehicle drivers, shunters and junior firemen, and later others whose work could be done by females. Young single women were also called up and a few of those, already in the company's employment from before the war, were drafted into the Women's Royal Air Force (WAAF), the Auxiliary Territorial Service (ATS) or the Civil Defence Services. Presumably, their work was done by hastily trained people brought in. Colleagues of those departing temporarily would often buy gifts and have a presentation to wish them well. Great Western men on active service made up a sizeable proportion of the Royal Electrical and Mechanical Engineers (REME). As time went on, the dilemma for the government was that although the criteria for retaining many skilled and qualified railway staff within 'reserved occupations' had to be amended to allow more men to join the forces, the importance of maintaining an efficient railway system at home was becoming more obvious. Petrol was rationed to everybody except the military, so the railways were carrying more goods than ever. This, together with millions of journeys being made by service personnel, it was hardly surprising the authorities wanted to stop unnecessary train journeys. The problems faced by the railway factories trying to meet government requirements for rolling stock with a depleted workforce were immense.

'Trip' was now cancelled, as were the Works outings, but railwaymen and women were still getting away. Peter Reade got three free passes a year and unlimited quarter fare by the company's trains. With some of his workmates, who now included ladies, he would often go up to the West End and see a show. Staff approaching retirement were asked to stay on. Some skilled railwaymen were loaned to outside firms, while outsiders arrived at the Works for the first time. A post was set up outside the station, specifically to direct war workers to their new lodgings. Later in the war, some skilled men were doing menial work with the forces, while their places on the railway were filled by 'dilutees' – outsiders with no experience. Men taken away from the department could apply for a 'Class B' release but later, after the invasion, the War Office also needed railwaymen to keep the railways working on the Continent. Swindon managed to avoid taking on munitions work at first; they got on with adapting the railway

A view from the drawing office files, showing air-raid damage. The official photographer is standing on the gasworks retort house looking east towards '24' shop and Ferndale Recreation Ground in July 1942. (Author's collection)

A production line making 1,000lb high-explosive bombs in the old 'points and crossings' shop. (BR National Railway Museum)

The carriage side canteen shortly after opening in 1943. (*GWR Magazine*)

for the expected conditions ahead. They undertook air-raid precautions, such as building shelters and fitting anti-glare screens to locomotives. Air-braking apparatus was fitted to the 2301 Class (Dean Goods) locomotives, which were expected to go to France with the British Expeditionary Force. Swindon also converted some carriages for casualty evacuation and ambulance trains. Eventually, due to the growing outside pressure, they fell into line with the other railway factories, which were making armaments. The usual suppliers of raw materials could no longer complete orders from railway companies, and Swindon was soon drawing on reserves or recycling their own. Waste produced by the Works, the scrap metal, wood shavings and sawdust, were all processed and re-used by the railway. Wastepaper, of which there was a huge amount, was re-used or cleared from all premises and sold to contractors. Supplies of quarto and foolscap paper were severly disrupted from the middle of 1939.

Numbers of workers were involved with the Local Defence Volunteers, later the Home Guard. These men would have to turn up for work the next morning, having been patrolling the Works and yards 'firewatching' half the night. In 1943, on account of its strength and importance, the GWR Home Guard Company was detached from the 5th Battalion and became the 13th Battalion commanded by Lt-Col. Dyer, a member of the CME's personal staff. By May of that year, 640 GWR men guarded Swindon Works and the surrounding railway premises. This figure rose significantly over the following year and did not include railwaymen in other local Home Guard companies. Jack Fleetwood thought the Luftwaffe had scored a direct hit on the foundry one particular day. Every so often a large brass cylinder was sent to Swindon to be scrapped. They came from Sudbrooke pumping station, where they were normally submerged in water causing them to become badly pitted and corroded. The deterioration caused water to get into the hollow chambers and Jack remembers one going into a 2-ton furnace which had not had the top cut off to drain the water out. The resulting explosion blew the top off the furnace and when the air cleared a bit, Jack could make out two fellas still standing next to the furnace where they had been working, having been showered in bricks and debris, but unharmed.

The Germans knew Swindon was an important railway centre and took aerial reconnaissance photographs, but they almost certainly did not know what else was being produced for the war effort. The workforce was constantly reminded of the need for discretion, particularly with regard to the movement of Government traffic. There were a few isolated attacks on the town by single enemy aircraft on their way home, either by strafing random targets or depositing their bombs from high altitude. Official sources say the railway town as a whole suffered 158 bomb alerts, 104 bombs, forty-eight people killed and 105 injured, of which thirty-three were seriously wounded. Fifty houses were destroyed or had to be pulled down and another 1,852 suffered some damage. The CME Dept only had to fill in a few craters in the Works' yards but a lot of railway families must have figured in these statistics. After Shorts Brothers Ltd of Rochester had been bombed in 1940, the company started production again in '24' shop and two other sites just outside Swindon. Built in 1929–30 for carriage repairs and painting, the massive '24' shop, with its extensive rail access, could normally hold 250 coaches. The work done here was considered low priority during wartime, so just two through roads were retained for carriage repairs. Another part of it produced shells and the rest was adapted for production of the tail sections of the new Stirling Bomber. Much of what went on in the new aircraft plant was, like all war work, kept quiet. Shorts was supposed to have been isolated within the railway works site. The workforce was issued with ID cards and had a separate entrance built for them. (It continued to be known as Shorts entrance until the Carriage Works closed in the 1960s.) In time, however, some of their work was being done by the nearby workshops and Great Western labour was being brought into '24' shop. One of the things people most remember about the displaced aircraft factory was the strong smell of dope that was sprayed on to the wings.

For some reason the CME Dept had been slow to start using female labour. Before 1942, women were taken on as porters, van guards, carriage cleaners, ticket collectors and other positions usually filled by men. Many of the ladies, when they did start coming in, had relatives 'inside' and this helped them to settle into the alien environment and break down any animosity towards them. They were at first put on light labouring or repetitive work and were soon doing semi-skilled machining and fitting. They proved to be equally good at light coppersmith and tinsmith work or as boilermakers and blacksmith assistants. Following conscription for women at the end of 1941, they came into the CME workshops in much greater numbers. They made up the labour shortage due to the combined effects of men being called up and the extra war work commitments. The general role of the newcomers was to supply and assist the skilled men and, with a few exceptions, they exceeded all expectations. Some went on to drive walking cranes and traversers and then the overhead cranes that ran up and down the length of some shops.

The workforce gave generously to the Comforts Fund, which the Staff Association had set up, with numerous branches around the system. The phrase a 'penny a week' was used to promote a Comfort Fund paybill deduction. The fund paid for parcels of such things as knitted clothing, cigarettes and a copy of the *GWR Magazine* to be sent to workmates on active service, as well as prisoners of war. In 1940 another of the schemes to help finance the war, The Spitfire Fund, was given a starting contribution of £500 from the directors. They knew that with the mood at that time, the company's employees would soon raise the £5,000 target; the theory being that the contributors were providing an extra fighter aircraft, which at the time was their only way of hitting back at the enemy. In an effort to encourage employees to buy defence bonds, the company offered interest-free loans, repayable via paybill deductions. They anticipated that a similar scheme to purchase the more popular 'national savings certificates' would create too much extra work for the already over-stretched paybill accounts staff, so stations, offices and depots were asked to set up their own national savings groups. It was pointed out that there was no setting up or running costs, and stationery (something the company was trying to cut back on) would be provided free. 'Lend to defend' was the catchphrase, and Swindon GWR had seventy-six national savings groups by the end of the war.

As a result of the extraordinary conditions brought about by the war, many traditions were discontinued, never to be reinstated. The foreman could no longer summarily dismiss a man. The dreaded discharges were a thing of the past and the smoking ban was lifted, with exceptions – probably as a concession for the introduction of the twelve-hour shifts. Promotions came along

A woman doing the job of 'hammer boy' early in the war. She controls the hammer blows delivered to an axle which the smith moves and turns to achieve the desired form. (BR National Railway Museum)

much quicker and even fashions seemed to be changing. Most photographs of the men we see today were taken in the 1920s or before, when virtually everybody wore ties and waistcoats, even on the shop floor. Jack said that 'apart from supervisory staff and management, most of the men were wearing their shirts open by the early forties. Overalls replaced the waistcoat and by the late forties one-piece overalls were popular'. From 1943 the men were represented by a joint Works Committee, formed of elected members of the NUR and the craft unions. The committee was an updated version of those already in place. Six members were elected from the full committee to meet with management and negotiate on all the prevailing conditions affecting the workers, excluding standard rates of pay. Mr H.C. Horrell, a patternmaker, was the first chairman of the Works Committee. In the 1950s he became the secretary. In exceptional circumstances, the committee was invited to send a deputation to speak with the general manager at Paddington. Most remember the local monthly meetings as the start of good labour relations, but some believed their negotiators became passive in the presence of the gaffers.

The 8750 0.6.0 Pannier tank engines were the only class of locomotives built throughout the war, but batches of mixed traffic and light passenger types were built. Not surprisingly, the '2884' heavy freight engines continued to be built until the government wanted all the railway works to produce a common type of freight locomotive. Starting in 1943, Swindon built eighty LMS 2.8.0 8F engines. They had already converted some of this class to oil fuel burning in 1941 for

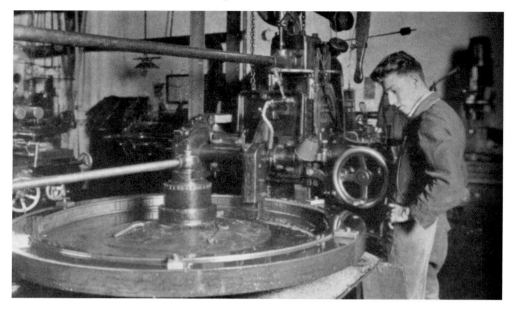

Cutting gear teeth on a turret ring for an armoured car. One of the first of the wartime contracts undertaken at Swindon for the Ministry of Production. (BR National Railway Museum)

Probably the most complex war work undertaken at Swindon was the 'multi-gun pom-pom' for the Navy. Some components were supplied by the Southern and the London & North Eastern Railways. (BR National Railway Museum)

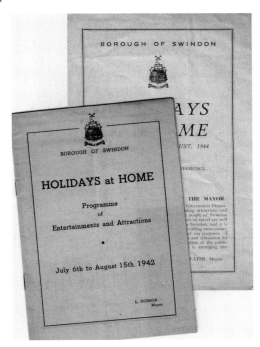

Programmes of events for 'Holidays at Home' during the war years 1942–44. (Author's collection)

use in the Middle East. Although the existing stock had to be patched up and sent back out, new wagons were built in large numbers throughout the war. Construction of new coaches was limited and then stopped altogether by 1942. Certain chemicals used in paints became scarce, so from 1942 express engines were painted in unlined green and all other types were painted black as they came through the Works. The chocolate and cream coloured coaches were painted over in brown, except for the stock of the *Cornish Riviera* and the *Torbay Express*. Vans were painted dark red and insulated vans a stone colour, and open wagons were not repainted at all. The Chief Mechanical Engineer, Mr Hawksworth, with the help of his draughtsmen, redesigned the mixed traffic Hall Class, the first of which appeared nameless in 1944. He then wanted to build a new type of express locomotive, possibly a *Pacific*, but the directors said no. Instead, he settled for a new two-cylinder 4.6.0., the first of which appeared in August 1945 – these were later named after counties on the GWR system.

The government introduced a number of schemes to improve the nutrition of the nation's workers. One was the expansion of industrial dining facilities. As a result, two new canteens opened in the Works – one on the loco side early in 1942 and one on the carriage side the following year. The latter was a completely new building between '15' and '21' shops. The small canteens and mess rooms, which served refreshments up until then, were retained. Before the war, there were no such facilities 'inside' because the majority of staff could not afford to use them. Many staff at Swindon could play musical instruments or entertain in front of an audience, so turns were put on in the new dining halls on Wednesday lunchtimes. In the early days especially, people were worried about the way the war might go and live entertainment made them feel better because they felt they were all in it together. Enid Hogden sang in a choir and they toured the workshops, singing at dinner time, which also helped keep up moral. By 1944, those in the Works and elsewhere in heavy industry were allowed extra rations, such as tea, sugar and cheese. Jack's mother often told him that 'it is a sin to give away your sugar allowance. People are dying bringing that across the sea'.

Peacetime showed little sign of improvement at first for the railway company. Docks, transport and miners' strikes meant a fuel crisis and shortage of raw materials. This then

One of two axle journal regrinding machines which also had provision for wheel balancing. (BR National Railway Museum)

The clean modern pattern shop in the late 1940s. (BR National Railway Museum)

caused a twelve- to eighteen-month waiting time for the supply of new machine tools. No less than anywhere else, the CME Dept was now struggling to catch up following the years of disruption to maintenance and new projects. Getting skilled labour demobilised and back into the factory was frustratingly slow. Therefore, staff that should have gone years before could still not be retired off. Rationing continued and in some cases worse than it had been during the war. Bert Harber said there was a general feeling that the depressed economy that the war had cured, would now return. On top of all this there was the most severe winter in living memory, starting in January 1947.

The railways, however, carried more people than ever before and Swindon Works was back to full production. Although with a further reduction in the working week, the department's aggregate production was, not surprisingly, down. The *GWR Magazine* tells us that for 1947 skilled labour was still down and semi-skilled and unskilled numbers were slightly up on the previous year. The Works undertook extensive re-conversion from large-scale wartime ordnance manufacture. Fifty-eight coaches from ambulance trains returned from the Continent to be made ready for ordinary traffic. Former restaurant cars were stripped at Swindon and reconditioned by contractors and military staff and mobile firefighting vehicles were converted back to peacetime use. The fuel crisis caused the company to undertake a regional scheme to power its locomotives by oil instead of coal. The CME Dept converted some of its locomotives and tenders to oil firing. They also sent out men to install oil storage plants at depots in South Wales, then in the South West. The scheme was short-lived, as the supply of oil, too, became difficult to obtain. By 1949 the locomotives affected had been converted back.

As had happened following the First World War, ceremonies were held in workshops on Sundays for the men in their number who never returned. Managers, the Mayor and Church dignitaries conducted services and would unveil memorial tablets; colleagues and relatives made up the congregation.

The chairman of the newly formed Railway Executive was bound to try to preserve morale on the eve of taking the railways into public ownership. He said 'every one of us railway men and women is now working in the direct service of our country, and all that Britain means to us and to the world is something worth working for'. It did little to alleviate the bewilderment and sense of loss felt by those who were fiercely loyal to the old Great Western. New staff coming in did not know any different, of course, and outwardly little did seem to change. The people in the offices seemed less disturbed by the change of ownership. Barbara Carter remembers having to wear a badge with B.R.(W) and a number on it, but otherwise 'everything carried on as normal', she said. No sooner had the cynical mutterings of the die-hards started to subside than the new regime of The Railway Executive (or was it 'The British Transport Commission', nobody was quite sure) started to make their mark. One of the changes that would later become apparent was that senior posts would be filled more and more by outsiders – a practice that was alien to Swindon which had thrived on a strong sense of loyalty and tradition. For instance, the top job went to Mr Smeddle in 1951. He had always been a LNER man but after 1948 he went to the Southern, then to Swindon. Mr Finlayson arrived from the Scottish region to be loco works manager in 1952. After four years he moved on to the London Midland Region (LMR).

Men have told me that the quality of materials coming in was often inferior or not what they were used to, due to alternative suppliers. Jack remembers:

The GW mixes we used to produce alloys in the foundry were light on tin. This did not adversely affect the castings and tin was expensive but, no, B.R. wanted the correct amount of tin in the mixture. This in itself was OK but now it did not suit the 'runners' and 'risers' [the channels] in our moulds. The size and shape of these channels, which let the molten metal in and the hot gases out, had been carefully worked out. The altered mix with the original moulds produced an inferior casting, but that was progress.

The need to replace ageing carriages, and make good losses suffered during the war, continued. The building programme proposed by the Western Region Executive in 1949 had to be cut back because of shortages of materials and limited workshop capacity. New wagons were also required in large numbers to modernise stock and reduce the heavy cost of repairs, but this too was frustrated mainly by shortages of steel. Unskilled foreign workers were bought in, mainly Poles, Italians and Ukrainians, under the government's work-permit scheme in response to the shortage of labour. Jack reckoned that more immigrants came into the foundry than to other shops, and at first they worked very hard. He said, 'We had two West Indians who were good workers but unfortunately one of them went mad and murdered his landlord, so we lost him.' George Petfield in the wages office remembers allocating a new pay number to a Ukrainian with the surname Lenik, 'He was the first one I remember. He started in the iron foundry around 1951.' The Western Region, and possibly the GWR before that, trained engineers at their works in Swindon from the developing countries of the Commonwealth. The Government London overspill scheme also brought some skilled and unskilled workers to the factory from the early 1950s. The newcomers described their new surroundings as 'out in the country', and they never missed an opportunity to ridicule the rural accent. The locals 'inside' renamed Thursdays 'pie day' in their honour.

In 1949 the loco works manufactured seventy-five new locomotives and undertook heavy and light repairs of more than 1,000 others in service. GW locomotive designs continued to be built under British Railways (BR), despite new standard designs being introduced. Some small GW 0-6-0 tanks were built until as late as October 1956. Trials took place between locomotives from each of the four main companies and a range of hybrid types emerged. The first of Swindon's BR designed locos, the 4.6.0 Class 4s, was completed in May 1951. They also built batches of 2-6-0s, including some of pure LMS design and 2-6-2 tanks, all mixed traffic types. Richard Woodley, an authority on Western Region locomotives, told me that the costs of building engines here was far higher than elsewhere. This was due to a shortage of skilled labour and reluctance by old hands to accept British Transport Commission (BTC) changes,

Above: Small brass plate from a bogie from one of the first D800 Warship Class diesels built at Swindon. (Author's collection)

Right: The driver's desk and control cabinet in the cab of Warship Class Loco D823. The date given for this photo is June 1960, some weeks before entering traffic. (Author's collection)

Opposite: The Works' principle officers in 1949. Back row, left to right: C.C. Teasdale, P.H.J. Woolfrey, S.A.S. Smith, H. Coltan, V. Hurle and G.W.G. Tew. Front row, left to right: C.T. Roberts, K.J. Cook, H. Randle and H.G. Johnson. (BR National Railway Museum)

designed to speed up production. 'Working to rule' was usually sufficient to get the men what they wanted. Richard said that although the loyalty and discipline of the old company had gone, the finished article was as good as, if not better, than the same product built at other railway works. The feeling amongst the men was that contracts were being diverted elsewhere mainly to Derby by the influential ex-LMS officials on the BR board. In 1957 a dispute over piecework caused the supply of components to the AE shop to be held up and some locomotives to be stuck there for extended periods; 5024 *Carew Castle*, for instance, went into the factory in April for a 'heavy general' overhaul. As with any class of overhaul where the boiler was taken off, this should have taken about twenty-eight days, but she was held there for more than five months. In 1956, Swindon completed the first heavy-freight class 9Fs. Freight engines were not normally named but the last of these was named, appropriately *Evening Star*. It was the last steam locomotive built for British Railways, leaving the Works in March 1960.

The biggest changes in the Works' history took place in the late 1950s with the transition from steam to diesel locomotive manufacture. The Works already had some experience with maintaining, repairing and building the mechanical parts of motive power worked by a four-stroke oil engine (diesel engine). In the 1930s, the GWR had received its first diesel shunters. They also brought in railcars to work some secondary routes. In 1948 a further six 0.6.0. diesel mechanical shunters entered service on the Western. This time they were partly built in the Works. Then there was the post-war experiments with gas turbine locomotives, as well as the cross country and inter-city diesel railcars of 1956. Swindon was one of three works required to start building the single- and multiple-unit railcars. At the end of 1957 more diesel shunters appeared. The following year the first mainline diesels were built here, at a cost of £120,000 (of public money) each. These were the warship diesels of 1958, based on the German V200 Class. The drawing office had the job of converting all the technical drawings into English but retaining metric measurements. The engine-transmission units, and other parts, were first imported from Germany then made under license in this country, with German engineers coming to Swindon to give assistance in the early days. The Western Region alone decided upon diesel hydraulics rather than diesel electrics, and

John 'Jack' Smithson working in the coppersmith's shop in about 1950. (Brian Smithson)

for some there was great pride taken in the new D800, with its impressive specification, something not seen since the first 'Kings' were built. Others would rather have waited for electrification, which, they were told, was to eventually cover the whole country.

The first alterations to accommodate the diesel-building programme was an extension to the carriage lift shop. This was for the manufacture of the railcars; a testing house for them was simultaneously built. 'A' shop was partially converted to the building and maintenance of mainline diesel hydraulic locomotives and 200hp diesel shunters. There were new sections for construction of bogies and repair of diesel transmissions, wheel assemblies and final drives. A new X-ray testing house was built in 1958 as a consequence of the widespread use of welded fabrications in diesel locomotives. X-ray pictures would show cracks and soundness of welded seams. The 'barn', the large shop between the Works' turntable and 'A' shop, where tubes had been removed from steam boilers, was now being taken over, in sections, as a diesel engine test house. 'W' shop, the machine shop associated with the manufacture of cylinders and main frames, was being converted for repair and testing of diesel loco air compressors and exhausters. The amount of work done in the foundry had started to decline dramatically, so half the total area was to be used for adjustments and painting of the new locos and to relieve the congestion in 'A' shop. This new section was to be set up under the direction of the ex-'G' shop foreman Mr Simpkins. The 'X' shop (points and crossings) had recently moved to a new building and the old shop became the 'ET' shop, to be fitted out for repairs and testing of motors, generators, dynostarters, control gear and other electrical equipment. Since October 1956, classes had been run in Emlyn Square to teach drivers and workshop staff the principles of the new locomotives. Mr Clark, the first tutor, said the courses for fitters were the longest and most involved.

Alan Lambourn worked on the D800 Warship Class in Peter Brettell's 'finishing off and trials gang' in 1959. Here, they took the locomotive outside to test and prime the two Maybach engines and Mekydro transmission units, cure leaks and bleed the injectors. Fitters on this work at that time were 'Dick' Gleed, John Bunce, John Dashfield, Arthur Cook, Bill

The replacement 'X' shop – points and crossings (trackwork) – on the north-east corner of the site. This was the last shop to be at the Works. It was used by the railway for just four years. (Ken Ellis)

Hobbs and Eric Turner. Two of them would also go out with the loco while it was tested on the mainline. To go 'on trial' with the engine you had been working on was always considered a bit of a privilege, and not just among apprentices. After the initial trials, the locomotive would work temporarily from Swindon shed, but still with one 'A' shop fitter and perhaps an apprentice in attendance. It would normally take over the 10.47 a.m. to Paddington and work the 2.00 p.m. parcels back. From leaving the factory to handing over to the traffic department, was usually between twelve and eighteen days.

The only electrical parts on a steam loco were the automatic train control apparatus, but the diesel building programme in the mid-1950s would require many more electricians. Seventy or eighty extra 'sparks' arrived from London and the Midlands during the initial diesel-building programme, although some went straight over to the carriage side. The Electrical Trades Union (ETU) was quite militant, or well organised, depending on your viewpoint. Consequently, their pay rates were higher, making them expensive to employ. 'Danny Lee and George Hall were the ETU shop stewards at that time and "Nobby" Clark for the electrical stores,' said Tony Huzzey. For other trades, Mervyn Hayward and Gordon Ing represented the coppersmiths and tinsmiths, Edgar Major the boilersmiths, Bill Peacey the vehicle builders and Jim Masters and Les Bates represented the fitter/erectors in the AEU. Terry Larkham was an NUR steward in the stores, and internal transport man Gordon Turner was works' convenor for the T&G WU. On the carriage side, George Scotford, Harold Sealy and Norman Piper represented the trimmers and upholsterers; Norman was the grandfather of actress Billie Piper. Reg Clark was steward in the C&W stores, Les Bates and Reg Clark had in turn been full-time chairmen of the Works Committee. Union men often became town councillors as well, and some went on to serve as Mayor.

By 1950 there were seven other major employers in the area, including four engineering firms. Through the decade, the railway works found it increasingly difficult to attract and retain both skilled and unskilled workers with yet more firms moving in to the area. In addition,

'K' shop – coppersmiths and sheet metal work – 17 March 1960. (R Grainger)

young men were required to leave temporarily for the two-year conscription. The majority of young family men who arrived in the town were attracted by better conditions in the car plants and electrical component industries. Peter Reade was typical of many railwaymen. He was attracted by the thought of higher wages elsewhere and was becoming worried by the rundown of his industry. 'Blacksmith's were no longer in demand, as forgings gave way to pressings in the new diesel manufacture. However, the better money never really happened because of industrial disputes in the car industry, and I regretted going,' said Peter. Despite massive post-war development and new industry, the railway works was still the town's biggest employer at the beginning of the 1960s. Thereafter, the railway industry declined locally and job losses were dramatic.

Some young men, yet to have financial commitments, were not necessarily attracted by the firms offering the highest wages. The railways still held a deep fascination and many young men were railway enthusiasts who just wanted to work on the railways. Bob Grainger was a trainspotter and photographer, and his introduction to a working life in the factory was not via the usual process. He did not live in the town, he lived in Cirencester, not far from the chairman of the British Transport Commission, Sir Brian Robertson. Bob wanted to work with his beloved engines, so his mother asked someone who knew the chairman to see if he would help. After contacting the boy's headmaster, Sir Brian gave Bob a letter to take to Swindon, which of course was enough to get him in. Unfortunately he found himself in the iron foundry office, learning to become a clerk. After much explaining, he was transferred to 'K' shop (coppersmiths) office until he started his apprenticeship on the loco side. 'All I remember about this office was the senior clerk, Mr Phillips, getting me to write out coal and slow combustion tickets, which were nothing to do with 'K' shop. My net pay then [January 1960] was about £3 15s,' said Bob.

II

OTHER CONSIDERATIONS

GETTING TO 'THE FACTORY'

Before the war most Swindon railwaymen walked to work. There were fourteen entrances around the 326-acre site. During normal working hours, the men had to use whichever entrance was nearest to their workplace. All men working nights and shifts booked on and off at the Works' gatehouses, where their name was required in the register. If they wanted a pass-out they got it from the time office; there was always someone there at night. In George's time, at least, the only gates manned and open all the time were the main tunnel and, further down the road, the C&W tunnel entrances: the Whitehouse Road/Beatrice Street entrance and the Bruce Street Bridge/gasworks entrance.

'The routes to the factory were always covered in spit. They used to have to hose the tunnel out every day. The state of the average workman's lungs was very poor,' said Jack. If you didn't know someone by name, then 'hello brother' was the usual acknowledgement before the war. Many of the older men touched their caps to the foreman if they passed him on the way to and from work. Bicycles were not permitted on the premises, so for a fee some people who lived near to the entrances of the factory allowed men to leave them in their back garden while the owner worked 'inside'. Doug Webb left his bicycle, complete with acetylene lamps, at the first house in Redcliffe Street. The going rate before the war was 3d a week, or 4d if the cycle was put in a shed. Mr Knee, the newsagent opposite the Bristol Street entrance, also made a few extra coppers by allowing cycles to be stored in his shop. Sometime in the early 1940s, cycle permits were obtainable and storage facilities provided. Then some trades, like electricians and plumbers, were even allowed to cycle around the Works in the course of their duties. In the 1950s, as well remembered, the wall of cyclists leaving the Works was formidable enough to stop the traffic in its path. Dave Viveash said that his chargehand, on the 'finishing off gang', Stan Lewington, rode a horse to work. 'He came across the fields from Lydiard and left the horse in an outbuilding near Even Swindon Farm, which was next to the Works' entrance in Redcliffe Street. Then he would work all day in his riding boots.

The Swindon Corporation Trams had finished for good in 1929 and fifteen double-decker buses took over the local services. After the war, and perhaps before, Swindon Borough Transport ran early morning buses on weekdays only. No times were given in the public timetable, so perhaps they were for railwaymen in particular. The other major bus company was Bristol Tramways, better known as the Bristol Bus Company. They also ran services in the 1950s 'from the Emlyn Square – GWR on days when the BRWR [British Railways Western Region] are open'. Before the war, most of the managers that lived any distance away would motor in and park in the fire station yard.

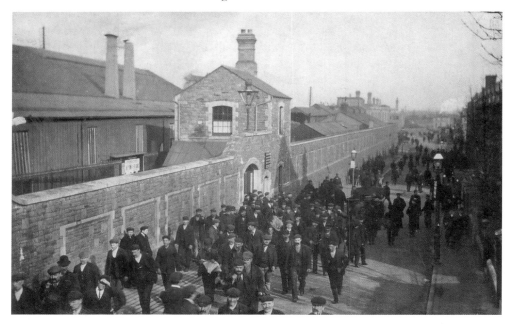

The carriage tunnel entrance in Station Road. The Junction Station is in the background. This view was taken near what was known by locals as Bullens Bridge, long after the bridge was removed in 1923. (Author's collection)

Quite a number of men and office women lived some distance away and had to travel in by workman's train. Services converged on Swindon junction from five different directions: Wootton Bassett, Chiseldon, Purton, Highworth and Cirencester. Old factory men still talk about the scramble to make the connection at Old Town Station (Swindon) in the 1950s. Two workmen's trains arrived from different directions: Chiseldon and Cirencester Watermoor, two minutes apart. Rather than reverse, the train from Cirencester connected with the other train; the workers had three minutes to cross the footbridge and continue down to Junction Station with the Chiseldon people. The train from distant Cirencester had started in 1925 when the Midland & South Western Junction Railway (M&SWJR) Works there was closed and the workers transferred to the GW Works. The last Christmas – in 1943 – before he left school, George Petfield was travelling from Wootton Bassett to Swindon to work as a temporary postman. He would catch the workman's train, laid on for factory workers. When it came to travelling Christmas morning, he was surprised to find it also ran that day, and 'it was quite full too'. Later, George used the 7.25 a.m. workman's train from Bassett regularly to get in to work, as did Peter Reade. Peter said, 'I cycled down from Broadtown and met George Evans on the way to the station. He was a bricklayer in the factory and we travelled in together'. A lot of women used the service to get to Wills's, Compton's and Garrard's, as well as those going to the railway works. People used the same compartment every day and newcomers were made to feel uncomfortable if they took someone else's regular seat. These trains were pulled by one of the modern pannier types, usually a 57XX Class and two to four non-corridor coaches, depending on the service. 'The secondary stock that was used was still gas-lit up until about 1945. There would be four on from Bassett and it was usually pretty full. The Purton train only needed two coaches,' said George.

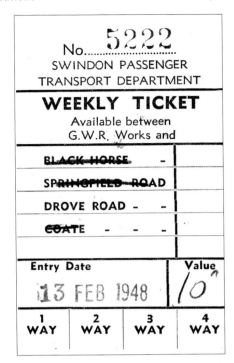

No. **5222**
SWINDON PASSENGER
TRANSPORT DEPARTMENT

WEEKLY TICKET

Available between
G.W.R. Works and

BLACK HORSE	-	
SPRINGFIELD ROAD		
DROVE ROAD -	-	
COATE -	-	-

Entry Date			Value
13 FEB 1948			10
1 WAY	2 WAY	3 WAY	4 WAY

A workman's weekly bus ticket from 1948, priced 10*d*.
The back is endorsed with a CME Dept, Swindon,
cash office stamp. (Author's collection)

THE MEDICAL FUND

The Great Western Medical Fund Society (MFS) facilities were available to railway workers in the Works, as well as their dependants and retired and widowed members. Apart from the war years, the membership was between 36,000–39,000 local people at any one time. Subscribers were offered a whole range of medical, surgical and health services. It is thought that no other similar scheme operated anywhere else in the country. George pointed out that people living outside the town could not make full use of the services offered, therefore he thought they may have paid a reduced subscription.

The Dispensary and Baths, the large building on the corner of Milton Road, also provided hairdressers and Russian and Turkish baths, as well as a tone up under the hands of an expert masseur. There were large and small swimming baths, which 'compare[d] favourably with any in the south-west'; one of which could be converted, after hours, into a dance hall or a rink for roller skating. The pool opened at 6 a.m. and some railwaymen would have a swim before work. During the war years, members of HM Forces, stationed in or near the town, were allowed to use the baths and washing facilities.

Many children of Swindon railwaymen were given a regular spoonful of cod liver oil, followed quickly by the far more pleasant brimstone and treacle, to help keep them healthy. Mothers collected these preparations in 2lb jars, which were available from the medical centre dispensary on prescription. Dr Gibson, the chief medical officer, and his team of ten full-time general practitioners, held surgeries here, morning and evening. They made domiciliary visits and provided an emergency call-out service.

The new Surgical Outpatients Department round the corner in Faringdon Road, known by locals as 'the surgery', treated mostly minor accidents from 'inside'. Crushed or lacerated hands were common, as were burns and foreign particles in eyes. Until the 1940s, this building at the top of Taunton Street had been divided up for various uses. The west end was the lime house;

the rest had been split between a garage for the MFS hearse, bath chairs and a rifle range. The horse-drawn hearse was provided by the Fund until the late 1930s; it was known locally as the 'Shillibier'. The adjacent hospital also served as a dressing station for casualties coming in from the factory. There was a fully equipped operating theatre but, despite the range of facilities, they could not always treat serious cases. Jack Sutton had been an ambulance inspector at Swindon since 1944, a full-time post probably created during that period when the ambulance organisation was enlarged. Mr Sutton's main role was to train the Works' first aiders, and this he continued to do for at least twenty years. Another of his duties, mercifully rare, was to accompany seriously injured workmen by train to one of the large London hospitals. The GWR had an arrangement with the Royal Westminster Ophthalmic Hospital and penetrating eye injuries were taken there. It was not unheard of for an up express to be stopped, especially to pick up badly injured men from the factory, and an ambulance to be waiting at Paddington.

The GWR cottage hospital was enlarged in 1927 with a temporary extension to become a forty-two-bed hospital. After other less ambitious plans had been explored, it was decided to build a new four-storey hospital on the site, doubling the existing capacity. However, the economic depression took hold and the new building plans were abandoned. Gwendolen Mercer began training as a nurse at the hospital in 1944. She said:

> I remember there were a lot of Welsh girls working at the hospital. There was a great sense of comradeship among the nurses [immediately after the war some patients remember there was quite a shortage of nurses]. We used to live in the nurses home in Emlyn Square and [were] only allowed out on our one day off a week. There were several sisters in the hospital, but the probationary staff still got to do a great deal of nursing. In our second year we were allowed to stitch and some nights there were only two of us left in charge of a ward. But Miss Wood, the matron, lived in and was never far away, although it was on pain of death if you called her in the night. We were not allowed out of the nurses home after 8 p.m., unless we had special permission.

Mr Greenwood, and in 1940 his former assistant Mr Schofield, were the general consulting surgeons. There were also doctors and consultants for orthopaedic, ophthalmic, dental and other specialities.

Ex-patients all said the hospital was spotlessly clean with a strong smell of antiseptic everywhere. Many remember being wheeled straight into the operating theatre with no pre-med, and seeing all the surgical instruments being laid out. A mask and a pad, soaked with ether, was held over your face and you tried to count up to ten. Afterwards most said they felt very sick. Children had tonsils removed and went home the same day but patients recovering from appendicectomy or hernia (rupture) repair were not allowed out of bed for three weeks. The local Methodist minister and the curate from St Marks came around to see inpatients regularly and the Salvation Army came in to sing hymns on Sundays. Visiting was on Wednesdays, Saturdays and Sundays, as well as public holidays. What food and sweets were given to the patients was strictly monitored. A period of convalescence in one of the jointly-run railway homes might be considered beneficial following inpatient care. The Great Western Medical Fund Society ceased to exist, upon the introduction of the National Health Act on 15 July 1948. At the date of dissolution, 18,000 members were entitled to shares, amounting to just over 2s for each complete year of unbroken membership.

MEDICAL CARE IN THE SHOPS

In theory, the safety equipment provided was leather aprons in the 'hot shops', welding shields and eye goggles. Men kept such things locked away for their own personal use, so newcomers might well have found them hard to come by. Ordinary window glass was the only suitable

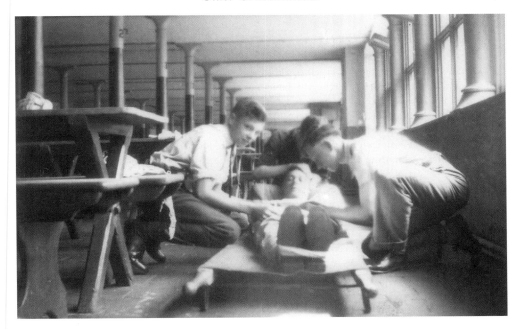

Ambulance training in the GWR mess rooms in London Street. A young Bert Harber acts as the casualty. (B. Harber)

transparent material available at the time but the goggles would stop a flying particle of some force. There were, before the war, 103 dressing stations (first aid posts) with a bell, with which the walking wounded could summon the first aider. In 1931 the staff magazine reported that 2 per cent of the Swindon workforce (270 people) were ambulance trained. This was amongst the lowest in the department. The man qualified to administer on the spot treatment in the foundry had a reputation for being heavy handed, so the casualties would get young Jack to treat them. He could remove a particle from their eye or clean and dress a cut with the minimum of discomfort, but this was highly improper and Jack was reported and told to stop. Serious accidents in the workshops were rare, but loose clothing becoming caught in the moving parts of machinery, or suspended loads slipping from lifting tackle, did sometimes cause serious injury.

Accident reports had to be made out and sent to the CME when a member of his department was injured at work. Where the company judged itself to have been negligent, a man would receive compensation equivalent to his wages for the period of his incapacity. This was subject to a doctor's report and sometimes the services of the company's own medical officer would be called upon to give a second opinion. If he was permanently incapacitated but still able to walk well, he might be invited to return to the Works to do menial work. One such fellow was employed to go round and clean all the phones with disinfectant; he would have been paid as a labourer. From 1949, if a man who had twenty-five years or more adult service was reduced in grade, owing to ill health or accident, he would receive the mean rate between the vacated post and the post to which he was reduced, up to a maximum loss of 10s a week.

During the early 1950s a rehabilitation workshop was set up at Swindon Works to assist the convalescence of injured workers. Under medical supervision, patients were put on light production work as physiotherapy. In 1957 two casualty centres were opened within the Works, one on the loco side and one on the carriage side, for treating injuries at work.

STEALING

There are numerous surviving stories of petty thieving and it was no doubt a major problem for the company. The stores department was allowed costs for the secure storage of materials and general supplies against pilfering. It went on at all levels, so it cannot be generally associated with hardship, even before the war. Jack's neighbour boasted of his ill-gotten gains once too often and his workmates convinced him the watchmen were going to pay him a visit one particular evening. He got a pass-out and hurried home to burn the plunder in the kitchen copper (you could burn anything in those things, said Jack). The fellow was being wound up but if he did take anything further, he never admitted it. For those who did a bit of model engineering or carpentry on weekends and used materials from the workplace, there was the constant risk of police spot checks. Tins of paint or tools were often seen hastily deposited along the exit approaches when word came back that searches were being conducted outside. At some stage the Works Committee had somehow managed to negotiate that they would receive prior warning when security purges would be carried out.

When the royal waiting rooms at Slough Station were no longer required for that purpose, several gangs of different trades on the carriage side were sent to clear them; this was about 1950. The royal furnishings and decoration came back to Swindon but much of it could not be sold, including the lavish carpet which one person took a fancy to. After cleaning, it was carefully folded, packed and put on a handcart and covered with a small amount of purchased wood. The paperwork handed in at 'Webb's entrance' described it as just a pile of blocks. After demobilisation, Doug Webb returned to the factory, stripping out coach interiors. Of course, he kept the coins found down behind the seats to supplement his labourer's pay. However, when he found a gold cigarette case in a royal coach, he handed it straight in and 'never thought of doing anything else'. Jack remembers that most of the men in the shops were very honest. Occasionally, however, he said tobacco or snuff would disappear from the line of jackets hanging up. Anyone caught would be outcast and have his working life, and possibly his life outside, made unpleasant by his fellow workers. If a man claimed to have lost his wages, a whip round was organised and would virtually cover his loss. Sadly, as time went on, it was suspected that this good will was being exploited and the practice gradually died out.

DISCIPLINE

According to the NUR conditions of service handbook for railway employees of 1937, a man charged with misconduct, neglect of duty or other breaches of discipline would be forewarned in writing of the nature of his offence and the punishment he was likely to expect. He was allowed to state his defence, call witnesses and advocate any extenuating circumstances before the company's officials, prior to a final decision being arrived at. At such an interview the accused could be accompanied by an advocate, usually a representative of his union. Where doubts arose or where the case(s) was sufficiently serious, it could be heard by a more senior official. If and when found guilty of a serious offence, he had the right of appeal to a superior officer and the reconsideration of the case. The company was keen to avoid appeals but in the event it should happen, it should be done before any punishment was handed out. The accused had to make an appeal in writing within seven days. He could, if he so wished, be heard again in person and accompanied by his immediate boss, a fellow workman or a representative nominated by the man's trade union. It was usual to allow a standard day's pay in cases of men attending disciplinary inquiries.

Although the railway companies must have agreed to the above, the GWR wording in the 'General Rules and Regulations' of the same period gives the accused little hope of a proper hearing. It states that they may at any time 'dismiss without notice' or 'suspend from duty, and after enquiry, dismiss without notice'. No doubt the company assumed the tone was sufficiently forthright to deter serious lapses in discipline, but still a man's whole livelihood was at the mercy of the foreman or overseer's attitude. This must have been particularly evident at times, when the company was looking to cut the workforce.

These then were the official processes. By the 1930s some wrongdoings were handled with a little more discretion. According to local folklore, when a Swindon engine driver was called to account and his story seemed far-fetched, his foreman, who had himself come up through the ranks, would interrupt with 'you tell me the truth, and leave me to tell the lies to the Superintendent'. Another unconfirmed story heard by George Petfield concerned a worker from the carriage side who was unhappy about his pay. He arrived at the wages office drunk, caused a scene and threw a punch at George Tomes, the senior clerk in carriage wages. He missed and ended up on the floor. This being the late 1940s, Mr Tomes exercised his authority and summarily suspended the worker for a week. Earlier in the century the various company rules on conduct also threatened fines and, in some cases, 'instant dismissal'. Jack said that in Great Western days, the local newspaper was regularly taken to the manager's office and scrutinised to see if any of the men had been in front of the magistrate. If they had, their names and details were recorded in a 'black book'. The book of names survives today but Jack can only speculate as to whether any further use was made of the entries.

ASBESTOS

The CME Dept used asbestos to lag its boilers, steam pipes and locomotive cylinders against heat loss. It was applied as a paste and when dry, clad with steel sheets. This method of insulation was uniquely very effective; asbestos does not deteriorate, nor does it corrode the steel around it, and is re-usable. One fellow worked in a corner of 'A' shop, breaking down used asbestos so it could be re-used. He was probably a 'green card man', said Dave Viveash. The railway, like all firms, was required to employ so many disabled people and that's what they were known as 'inside'. Before asbestos was mixed to a workable consistency, it released fine particles into the air when disturbed. This was particularly so when it was being removed after use. Workers inhaling particles would develop some scarring of the lining of the lungs but there were usually few troublesome symptoms initially. Wives of these men were at risk too, when washing the dusty overalls.

Because it was many years after exposure before a person became unwell, it took a long time to make a connection between asbestos and serious lung disease. It was well into the 1960s before it was generally accepted that these people had a high risk of developing lung cancer, especially mesothelioma. Not until then were precautions offered against the inhalation of particles. It was suspected for some time that there might be a parallel between asbestos and another mineral, silica, used elsewhere in industry. The damage to the lungs of long-term exposure to the latter had been acknowledged long before. Because of the high incidence of works' men presenting with symptoms, the disease became known locally as the 'Swindon disease'. George Petfield remembers paying out in 'A' shop on summer evenings when the sun's rays shone across the shop. He said, 'You could see the air was full of dust.' No doubt, some of that dust came from stripping or reconstituting asbestos and, as it turned out, this was not the only dangerous place to work. Jack said: 'Because of the finer particles, blue asbestos was more dangerous. It was sprayed onto carriage bodies in later years. The train heating pipes were wrapped in asbestos tape.' In the early 1960s, Swindon started using polyurethane rigid foam to insulate its carriages against noise and heat loss. Diesel hydraulic locomotives were insulated with fibre glass.

UNDERGROUND FIRES

Much of the land that the Works stood on had been built up to a height of between 12-20ft. Coke, cinders and clay were used over large areas to the west and to the north of the site and pockets would burn, following spontaneous combustion. Underground fires would burn slowly and spread. The ground reached temperatures of 500°C and the clay turned to brick. Sometime after the war, the Works fire brigade had sunk pipes down and saturated the ground for weeks on end. Mr Sealy, the Works' fire officer, said years later that 'the heat travels through concrete and steel very quickly and no amount of water will touch it. The only way to stop it is to remove it'. Vague references have been made about the fires since at least as early as the 1920s by employees, but I could not find anything recorded on the matter until the 1950s. The *Western Region* magazine said one area had been burning continuously for twenty-five years and contractors had recently been bulldozing down to the original ground level. Bert Harber remembers trenches they made being filled with sand to try to contain the spread. His father, a first aider, was sometimes summoned to Redcliffe Street Bank because men working there had been overcome by fumes. In the early 1970s the potential for problems caused by this phenomenon to buildings and service mains was found to be considerable.

LEISURE TIME

ORGANISED LEISURE ACTIVITIES

With active co-operation of the company, a highly organised and competitive programme of leisure activities developed over the years. Leagues for team games were organised at local and company level by the Social and Educational Union (S&EU), which became the Staff Association in the mid-1930s. It was later claimed that the GWR S&EU (SA) was the largest industrial organisation in the world at that time. The newly appointed assistant to the CME, Mr F.W. Hawksworth, became the Swindon branch president in 1932, the year they moved to a new headquarters, the Bridge Street Institute. With the move, they inherited an integral theatre with seating for 180 people, albeit rather cramped and dilapidated. It was soon modernised so the Great Western Players, the aptly named dramatic section of the 'Association', could put on their full and one-act plays there. The Swindon branch of the GWR S&EU (SA), which had evolved from the old Temperance Union, had an impressive 4,000 members in the 1930s. The Mechanics Institute was the home venue for most of the indoor competitions. Skittles and whist drives were perhaps the most popular team games. For the less energetic, there was arts and crafts or horticultural shows, amongst other diversions. Outdoor sports, such as football, cricket, hockey, bowls, miniature rifle practise and tennis were played at the GWR (Swindon) Athletic Association sports ground, which opened in 1931.

Like the other large GWR centre at Paddington, Swindon too had respected classical and light operatic groups made up of singers and choruses, musicians and actors from amongst the Works' staff. Regular musical programmes were put on in the Mechanics Institute Concert Hall, which included songs, soloists, choruses and humour, as well as the famous Swindon 'Gleemen' male voice choir. Many of these, and other classical and modern musical turns performed by railway workers, ensured Swindon put up a strong showing at the Music and Drama Festival and took a high proportion of the prizes.

The first full-length operas at the Mechanics Institute Theatre started in 1930. Less than two weeks after the final performance that year, the building suffered a major fire. Renovation was completed in 1932 and the theatre reopened as the Playhouse; now the building had a concert hall and a dance hall. By the 1950s, the Playhouse was equipped with facilities easily equal to any provincial theatre. The Swindon College, Choral and Orchestral classes, which became the Swindon Music Society, gained respect throughout the music world for attempting the lesser-known operas, rather than staying safe with the popular productions. Jack Winter (bass baritone) and Ray Hatherall (tenor), together with his wife Lorna Cantor, were the best-known names from the 1930s through to the '50s. 'Jack worked in "No.1" accounts office and Ray was in "W" shop on loco frames,' said George Petfield. Mr Hatherall was responsible for

The Mechanics Institute's main building in the 1930s. (BR National Railway Museum)

Mechanics Institute council members' badge. (Author's collection)

The Great Western Silver Band outside the Mechanics Institute. Mr Alder was the conductor from 1930 until at least 1946. (Author's collection)

first bringing the Russian operas to England and having them performed at the Mechanics Institute. Soon the outside world heard about what was going on in Swindon and VIPs, such as composers William Walton and R. Vaughn Williams, were attending the shows, as was the head of the Royal Ballet. Despite the obvious home-grown talent, the theatre never managed to pay its way.

When performances were suspended during the war, operatic singers and musicians set up their own travelling concert party in their spare time called The Gay Cravats. Doug Webb played the accordion and joined Bert Fluck's concert party in the late 1930s when he was only in his late teens. He remembers the group included Alf Salter, a baritone singer who worked in 'W' shop, comedian Jack Wilkes, Beryl Done and Ivy Plyer, singer and comedienne respectively. George remembers that 'Bert was a nice chap. He played piano and entertained workers in the canteen during the war.' As a piano accompanist, his name appears in countless local and company-wide concert programmes, as does Iris Rainger of the General Stores Office. By the time Mr Fluck had taken over the running of one of the two main mileage offices from Harold Lewis, his daughter Diana Dors was regularly appearing in the top British films of the time (1946–48). Gwendolyn Binks worked in the CME offices for a time in the 1930s and '40s, possibly as a secretary in the motive power office on the ground floor. She, too, was the mother of a famous showbiz person – musician Justin Hayward. Beryldene Hunt was a name I kept seeing in surviving concert programmes and cast lists of local stage productions, as was Mavis Gilbey from the correspondence office. As everyone in the offices knew everyone else, I asked Barbara Carter if she knew Ms Hunt. She said, 'Oh yes, she worked in our machine room. Beryl lived for amateur dramatics. She was a real eccentric and even at work was rather theatrical'. Beryldene produced and acted in plays, was an elocutionist and gave concert recitals.

MECHANICS INSTITUTE

Besides the most popular attraction, the free holiday travel, the Mechanics Institute offered a lending and reference library, the only one in the town until 1943. The library held about

The Staff Association billiards and snooker team outside the Mechanics Institute in the late 1950s. The only people identified are Bill Hockin, Doug Mayhew, Ben Blackman, John Webb and Len Sweet – third, fouth, fifth, sixth and twelfth from left, standing. (Author's collection)

40,000 books and was open to non-members. Alongside were reading rooms, which included a table reserved for wives and daughters of members. Visitors talk of the sense of quiet and tranquillity in these parts of the building, contrasting with the din of the factory nearby. With its polished tables, ornamental ceilings and classical plaster busts, the interior resembled a grand country house rather than a works recreational centre. There was a smoking room, lecture hall and facilities for billiards, table tennis, chess and draughts. Upstairs was a theatre large enough for 800 people, which was also used for dances. Management was in the hands of an elected council of foremen and others. The Institute also had branches with reading, recreational rooms and libraries in the Gorse Hill and Even Swindon districts of the town.

This grand Victorian building had very churchlike architecture and a well-known brass weather vane on top of one of the two towers. The vane was quite clearly in the shape of one of Mr Dean's handsome 'single' locomotives, and unlike the one seen on the borough coat of arms, had not been divorced from its tender. After 1945 the facility, designed for the expectations of people 100 years earlier, was struggling to attract sufficient membership. By the 1950s the concert hall was used for any local events that needed a venue and other parts of the building were being used for storage.

THE ANNUAL DINNER

With great skill and enthusiasm, the 'organisation secretary' instilled motivation where necessary, and collected money for the 'Annual Dinner' and social evening, as well as the 'outing' to the seaside or inland beauty spot. These events were a traditional part of most offices and shops throughout the department. The foremen and the inspectors also had their

A C&W foreman's outing, about 1930. Richard Dening, a head foreman, is front right. (B Carter)

annual get-togethers, as did some retired groups of workers. A write-up of the larger occasions would often appear in the local evening paper.

George's office would go to a local inn, such as The Crown at Stratton or the White Hart at Cricklade, for their staff Christmas dinner. This was arranged for an off-peak period during work time. A Corporation bus, usually a single-decker, was hired for the occasion. Annual dinners were popular inside and outside the Works in those days, so it was sometimes not possible to book at a specific venue on a specific date. Therefore, they were not necessarily Christmas events but normally arranged for the autumn or wintertime. Surviving programmes show that most, if not all, local hotels catered for these occasions. The 'Chief' (CME) and all his personal staff held their Annual Dinner at the Goddard Arms Hotel, in the ballroom. Senior accounts staff were invited to attend, as were retired VIPs, but women were not. A professional photographer was invited along to take the customary group picture, and we can see from these that upwards of sixty people were invited and expected to attend. After the meal, toasts were made to the King or Queen and to the GWR company, interspersed with a programme of light entertainment, such as humorous songs, sketches and monologues. All the turns would have been performed by men from that department, and perhaps the reason the female employees were not invited was because some of the entertainment would have been considered unsuitable.

THE OFFICE OUTINGS

The 'outings' were the highlight of the office social activities and the best supported. Normally in June, this annual day would usually include a pre-booked dinner in the evening and often luncheon en route. The office calendar was always marked well in advance, as was the holiday period in July. Along with the annual holiday, outings were not arranged during wartime. Programme cards were printed and distributed, giving the travel arrangements, the menus, and organising committee members' names. Some of the party would ask everybody to sign their programme and they would be kept as a souvenir and reminder of the day. All the seaside resorts and places of interest between the South East and the South West were destinations for consideration; they were traditionally men or ladies only. The itinerary was usually fairly hectic. In 1936, '41' office visited the Colchester and Clacton area. The area east of London was always popular with the men, perhaps because of the chance to travel out of Liverpool Street or Fenchurch Street stations – these were the days when our railway system was of particular interest to a lot of men, especially railwaymen. Sometimes travelling via the capital included a West End show, on the way home.

The combined drawing office and the estimating office outings were on a Friday in June each year. In 1948 they bussed to Southampton for the Isle of Wight. The journey was always considered an enjoyable part of the day out, so on another Isle of Wight outing they went by train via Portsmouth and Southsea for the steamer crossing. The day was usually a long one, but with so many departments to accommodate in the month and the company insisting they be staggered, not everyone could get away on Fridays. Some offices and departments had been having an annual works outing since the 1890s, and quite possibly earlier. The locomotive managers' office outings started in 1905 and from 1924 the ladies of the typist section in that office took their 'day out' the same day. From surviving group photos, it is obvious that a river trip up the Thames from Caversham Bridge was a favourite for many shops, departments and offices, although that was probably the furthest the professional photographer was prepared to travel from his studio in Swindon.

George Petfield remembers the outings from 1948. They travelled mainly by train. The South Devon resorts or Minehead via Taunton were popular. The party would catch the 7.25 (5.30 Paddington) Penzance, via Bristol, train. Some would bring bottles of beer and it was a point of honour to sink the first pint before reaching Rushey Platt. There was a lot of drinking done throughout the day but George doesn't ever remember any rowdy behaviour. Among the places visited in the late 1940s and early '50s were Torquay, with a boat trip to Teignmouth for the pre-booked evening meal. In 1950 it was Sidmouth, with a meal in the upmarket Fortfield Hotel, and another time it was Weymouth. When returning from the South West, a Swindon Works party might have a private carriage, sometimes an open saloon attached to the rear of an up train. At Taunton, the carriage, upon returning late, as normal, was transferred to the 11.20 p.m. Taunton-Wolverhampton parcels. Sometimes a carriage for a homeward ladies outing was also attached here. One year, one of the vans on George's train developed a 'hot box'. He said, 'you could see flames coming from underneath just short of Frome'. Under normal circumstances they were due into Swindon Junction at 1.24 a.m. There were some very tired-looking men in the office the next day. George lived at Wootton Bassett until 1955 and sometimes if the train slowed down through that station, he and others from the town would risk jumping onto the platform, thus saving the late-night journey back from Swindon.

On their way to Eastbourne in 1949, the nearest thing to rowdy behaviour in George's party happened on a London bus between Paddington and Victoria. As they passed the Royal Artillery Monument, one of the day trippers, Frank Witts, who felt he could identify with this heroic regiment due to his First World War service, leapt up and tapped the window with his walking stick. The window smashed, showering everybody with glass. Brighton was another favourite destination. Then the meal was taken on the journey down on the Brighton Belle for 2s 6d a head. In the mid-1950s, the large party was walking from Brighton Station to the seafront and one of the locals enquired if they were on a demonstration.

Barbara Carter remembers her office outings being in May. She said, 'They were always on a week day, the company giving the staff the day off.' As with the men, the company gave the party free passage by their trains, which did not affect the free pass entitlement. Although they did not pay for any connecting coach or boat journey at the other end. In the late 1940s

The '21' office ladies' outing to Southsea in 1953. In the photograph can be seen Dot Woodham, Yvonne Hodey (*née* Jones), Jennifer Allen, Jean White, Madge Lilley (*née* Hartley), Mo Buckland, Mrs Beckington, Florence Brunger and Muriel Whale, from the mileage office. One or two others were from other offices. (Y. Hodey)

The 'No.40' office outing to Hunters Inn on Exmoor in 1949. Standing second from left is Jean Claughan. Sitting, left to right: -?-, Mary Shergold, Marjorie Gooding, Grace Turner, Gladys Ackrill, Barbara Carter (*née* Dening), Phyllis -?-. The lady on the far right lived in Drove Road and Barbara remembers her getting a message at work in August 1942, telling her to go home urgently, as her house had been bombed. (B. Carter)

the ladies of 'No.40' office visited such places as Hunters Inn, on Exmoor, the Isle of Wight and Minehead, which was the most popular destination. Yvonne Hodey only went on one outing, on a Friday in June 1953, when the ladies of '21' office went to Southsea. The last of the sponsored (office) outing's were in 1964, when the CME Dept became part of British Rail Engineering Ltd. That year George's lot went to Minehead, then on to Dunster by bus for the meal on the way home.

THE SHOP OUTINGS

In Jack Fleetwood's shop the men paid in to a fund throughout the year. This covered the transport and the beer. The foremen didn't come along in the early post-war days. They knew they needed to keep a distance from the men so as not to feel uncomfortable maintaining discipline at work. We always hired a motor coach, Jack said. 'If we used our free pass on train, they were funny about the beer [as already stated, this was not George's experience]. On the bus we could take all we liked.' Workshop outings were taken on Saturdays, as they were not given a day off by the company, and as a consequence, not all shops took an annual day out. Moulder Reg Dixon staggered off the bus at Portsmouth one year and laid on the grass. 'Pick me up on the way back,' he said. After a day on the Isle of Wight, they found him still laying in the same spot on the way back. One 'kiddie' the chargeman labourer always finished the evening with sea legs due to his affinity with Newcastle Brown, said Jack. 'The driver would put him off outside his house in Faringdon Road. We would get him to his door, ring the bell and run,' he said. Jack had always referred to his workmates as 'kiddies'. This was not a Swindon term, so he probably picked it up from his mother, who was a cockney. As with George's outings, Jack maintained there was never any bad behaviour – a few slightly bawdy songs on the bus perhaps, but that was all. He said, 'Sometime later, the coach company wanted to discourage the drinking on its tours; that, together with the increased ownership of private cars, killed off the "annual workshop day out".'

Before the war, the '15' shop outings were called 'the golden road' because they used to go to London with the option of going on to the FA Cup Final. In the 1950s Harry Bartlett still remembers Ron Franklin coming round for the 6d a week towards the outing and calling it 'the golden road'. By then they could only get blocks of tickets for the Amateur Cup Final. Bert Harber said that by the 1950s, the electricians' outings included the wives and children. 'Sapperton Woods was one destination I seem to remember,' he said.

'TRIP' – THE ANNUAL HOLIDAY

In the 1930s the Works closed at midday on the first Thursday in July for the holiday, and reopened the following Monday week. The local schools too broke up at midday on 'holiday Thursday'. The directors of the company provided the so-called 'free holiday trains', which took Swindon factory workers away for a well-earned break. Long-distance trains were made up of corridor stock and left on the Thursday evening travelling overnight; the rest left early the following morning. 'Trip Day' for railway people was the Friday and for the outside traders and others, it was the following Wednesday.

Bookings had to be made by the end of May and then details of the holiday train were displayed on the noticeboards. The local paper also published a summary of numbers travelling. In the week leading up to the holiday, the passes were collected from the Mechanics Institute; the travellers having already submitted details of their chosen destination and time they intended to be away. Also collected were tickets for relatives and friends of employees not entitled to free or privileged tickets. The CME Dept was responsible for the travel arrangements, which they passed on to the secretary and council of the Mechanics Institute. They dealt with the

Above: The '15' shop outing sometime in the early 1950s. 'Probably a lunchtime stop en route to Southsea,' said Harry Bartlett. Back row, left to right: coach driver 'Wacket' Giles, Frank Anderson, -?-, Norman Duffill, Roy Firth, George Kimber, Terry Buckland, Jack Perry, -?-, Maurice Dixon, Les Pinnock, -?-, Norman Rushen, Bill Sowden. Middle row, left to right: Dennis Male, Harry Lang, Alan Davis, Sam Harris, Ted Randall, Phil Pinchin, Stan Webb. Front row, standing left to right: Dick Jones, Howard Hopgood, -?-, Jack Wickendon, Keith Freeman, Harry Bartlett; Front row, sitting left to right: Les Hurst, Bob Comley, Dennis Holloway, Mervyn Stratford, Bernard Rawlings. (H. Bartlett)

Right: One of a series of Edwardian postcards illustrating the plight of Swindon families who dared to take a holiday, courtesy of the company. (Author's collection)

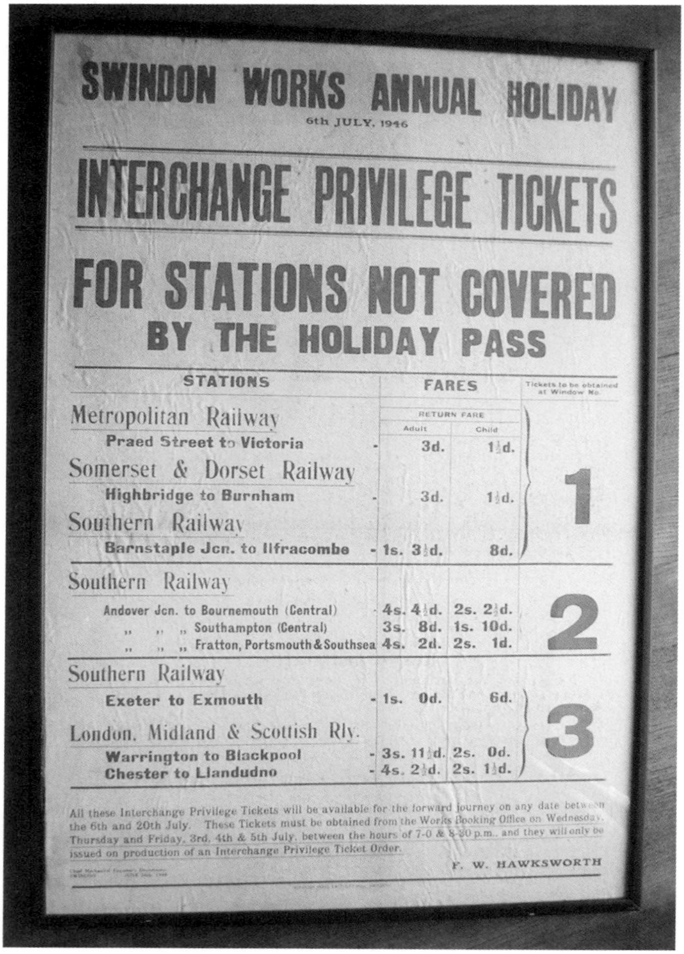

SWINDON WORKS ANNUAL HOLIDAY

6th JULY. 1946

INTERCHANGE PRIVILEGE TICKETS

FOR STATIONS NOT COVERED

BY THE HOLIDAY PASS

STATIONS	FARES		Tickets to be obtained at Window No
	RETURN FARE		
	Adult	Child	
Metropolitan Railway			
Praed Street to Victoria	3d.	1½d.	
Somerset & Dorset Railway			1
Highbridge to Burnham	3d.	1½d.	
Southern Railway			
Barnstaple Jcn. to Ilfracombe	1s. 3½d.	8d.	
Southern Railway			
Andover Jcn. to Bournemouth (Central)	4s. 4½d.	2s. 2½d.	
" " " Southampton (Central)	3s. 8d.	1s. 10d.	2
" " " Fratton, Portsmouth & Southsea	4s. 2d.	2s. 1d.	
Southern Railway			
Exeter to Exmouth	1s. 0d.	6d.	
London, Midland & Scottish Rly.			3
Warrington to Blackpool	3s. 11½d.	2s. 0d.	
Chester to Llandudno	4s. 2½d.	2s. 1½d.	

All these Interchange Privilege Tickets will be available for the forward journey on any date between the 6th and 20th July. These Tickets must be obtained from the Works Booking Office on Wednesday, Thursday and Friday, 3rd, 4th & 5th July, between the hours of 7-0 & 8-30 p.m. and they will only be issued on production of an Interchange Privilege Ticket Order.

F. W. HAWKSWORTH

Poster for the annual holiday in 1946, giving additional details for those visiting resorts in other railway companies' territories. It is unusual not to have the company name or initials displayed. (Author's collection)

publicity and bookings, and issued the passes and the travel details. The holiday pass covered travel to any of the seaside resorts on the Great Western. The nearest resorts of Weston and Weymouth were the most popular for day trippers, and Devon and Cornwall were easily the most popular areas to spend the week away. According to the *GW Magazine*, 27,416 people left the town in thirty-one trains in 1933, over 1,000 more than the previous year.

'Trip' was the most important leisure event of the year for the majority of the families in Swindon. The exodus of the townspeople in July was on such a scale that everybody in the town, whether they participated or not, have memories of 'Trip'. I have heard elderly residents in places such as Exmouth and St Ives still refer to early July as 'Swindon Week'. Because of the numbers of people and trains to be got away in a short space of time, the departure points varied – most left from the Junction Station, where even the local branch platforms were used. One or two trains bound for the South Coast left from the station in Old Town and meandered down the M&SWJR, as it was still called. The remainder were all west of

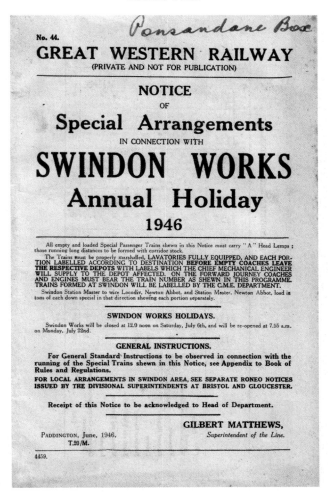

Ponsandane Box

No. 44.

GREAT WESTERN RAILWAY
(PRIVATE AND NOT FOR PUBLICATION)

NOTICE
OF
Special Arrangements
IN CONNECTION WITH
SWINDON WORKS
Annual Holiday
1946

All empty and loaded Special Passenger Trains shewn in this Notice must carry "A" Head Lamps ; those running long distances to be formed with corridor stock.

The Trains must be properly marshalled, LAVATORIES FULLY EQUIPPED, AND EACH PORTION LABELLED ACCORDING TO DESTINATION **BEFORE EMPTY COACHES LEAVE THE RESPECTIVE DEPOTS** WITH LABELS WHICH THE CHIEF MECHANICAL ENGINEER WILL SUPPLY TO THE DEPOT AFFECTED. ON THE FORWARD JOURNEY COACHES AND ENGINES MUST BEAR THE TRAIN NUMBER AS SHEWN IN THIS PROGRAMME. TRAINS FORMED AT SWINDON WILL BE LABELLED BY THE C.M.E. DEPARTMENT.

Swindon Station Master to wire Locodiv, Newton Abbot, and Station Master, Newton Abbot, load in tons of each down special in that direction shewing each portion separately.

SWINDON WORKS HOLIDAYS.

Swindon Works will be closed at 12.0 noon on Saturday, July 6th, and will be re-opened at 7.55 a.m. on Monday, July 22nd.

GENERAL INSTRUCTIONS.

For General Standard Instructions to be observed in connection with the running of the Special Trains shewn in this Notice, see Appendix to Book of Rules and Regulations.

FOR LOCAL ARRANGEMENTS IN SWINDON AREA, SEE SEPARATE RONEO NOTICES ISSUED BY THE DIVISIONAL SUPERINTENDENTS AT BRISTOL AND GLOUCESTER.

Receipt of this Notice to be acknowledged to Head of Department.

GILBERT MATTHEWS,

PADDINGTON, June, 1946.   *Superintendent of the Line.*
T.20/M.

4459.

Booklets were issued to officials, all down the line, giving instructions for the working of Swindon Works' holiday trains. This booklet was issued to the signalman at Penzance in 1946. (Author's collection)

England-bound trains which left from works' sidings on the down side of the mainline. Local trains and buses were run to connect with the holiday trains, bringing people in from outlying districts.

Although the town was noticeably quieter, not everyone was away at 'Trip'. Those people not going would often stay up or get up early to wave their neighbours off. 'The key's through the letterbox on a piece of string… Don't forget to feed the budgie, will you.' That's assuming the bird and cage were not going too! Local grocers' shops stayed open late before Trip Day and Trip Week and they often took the opportunity to close when the day trippers were away as shoppers were few and far between. Barbara Carter was a child in the 1930s who stayed at home. She said, 'My father was a clerk in charge of an office, and so as to offset the exodus somewhat, senior staff worked through the holiday. All I remember is how quiet it was everywhere and how difficult it was to get groceries'. Everyone wore their best clothes. If you were going to buy something new, you did so just before 'Trip'. Fashions inevitably

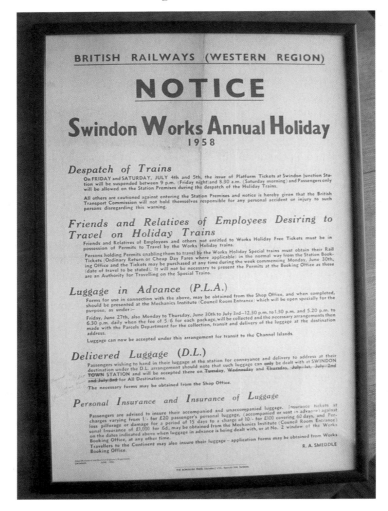

Presumably this 1958 poster was an office copy, as some details of the
direct luggage arrangement have been amended in pen. (Author's
collection)

changed slightly over the years. Before the war, the men wore a suit and usually a bowler hat
or straw brimmer. They might wear a bow tie and a handkerchief in the top pocket or perhaps
a buttonhole flower. The young men usually wore an open-neck white shirt and some took
their bicycles with them. For the ladies, a gaily patterned cotton dress and a raincoat, just in
case; 'gran' would of course wear her best hat. It was a great novelty for all the family to enter
the Works' premises at the Park Lane and Station Road entrances and walk along next to the
mainlines which were temporarily roped off. Climbing wooden steps into the waiting coaches
is remembered by many to this day, thanks partly to the often published official photographs.
Jack Fleetwood remembers some foundrymen that had cast their own carriage keys. They
would arrive a bit early to let themselves, their families and perhaps their friends in and have
a compartment for themselves.

By the late 1930s, with the start of paid holidays for the factory, the holiday break started
after work on the first Saturday in July. In 1939, with the population of Swindon at 63,000,

about 27,000 people filled the thirty Works' holiday trains and another 600 or so went by ordinary trains. With such statistics it should be remembered that a good proportion of the holidaymakers came from the area's surrounding borough. Many workers and their families were just getting used to the idea of staying away for the whole week when 'Trip' was cancelled from the first July of the war and for the duration. Perhaps the splendid planning used to get so many evacuees away from west London and elsewhere in such a short period owed something to Swindon Works' holiday trains. During the war, the factory did not close completely for the week. The holiday periods were staggered throughout July, August and September to keep production moving. People were discouraged from travelling and the borough council arranged a programme of entertainment and attractions, known as 'Holidays at Home' in the summer, starting in 1942.

After the war, the Works continued to close at 12 noon on Saturday, but now for two weeks. The last Trip train that day was away from Swindon by early evening; a few more trains left on the following Sunday, Monday and Tuesday. When the Saturday shift was dropped, the overnight trains for West Cornwall and north-west England left Friday evening; the rest early on Saturday, Monday and Tuesday. The burden of running all the extra trains (twenty-seven in both directions in 1946, and not all the trippers travelled by special trains) was shared by the Traffic Department and the CME Dept. The Swindon shedmaster would put loco's aside at the running shed for some time prior to Trip.

In 1950 the holiday shutdown was brought forward a week but returned to normal the following year. By now, because of nationalisation, the free tickets could take you all over the UK and Eire. Most people, however, continued to visit resorts that the old GWR Co. had promoted. By 1954 it was said that only about 50 per cent of people in this country went on holiday by train. This was not the case among Swindon railway families. Numbers varied little since the 1930s, but after 1956 there was reduction in the services due to trippers being diverted onto ordinary train services. Although the Works was showing no sign of the coming decline in 1957, the *Evening Advertiser* reported that the excitement of the annual holiday was not what it used to be. Locals seeing friends and relatives away said many looked noticeably less enthusiastic than they used to. Perhaps they had heard of the bus strike that awaited them on their return. The 'holiday specials' finished in the early 1960s. Swindon Works holidays are well remembered today because, like the children's fête, also organised by the committee of the Mechanics Institute, it captured the imagination of the children who grew up in an era when their memories were to be sought and recorded.